SUPER SIMPLE
COOKING FOR KIDS

SUPER SIMPLE COOKING FOR KIDS

LEARN TO COOK WITH 50 FUN AND EASY RECIPES FOR BREAKFAST, SNACKS, DINNER, AND MORE!

JODI DANEN, RDN

PHOTOGRAPHY BY EVI ABELER

ROCKRIDGE
PRESS

For general information on our other products and services or to obtain technical support, please contact our Customer Care Department within the United States at (866) 744-2665, or outside the United States at (510) 253-0500.

Rockridge Press publishes its books in a variety of electronic and print formats. Some content that appears in print may not be available in electronic books, and vice versa.

Interior and Cover Designer: Michael Patti
Art Producer: Sara Feinstein
Editor: Cecily McAndrews
Production Editor: Matt Burnett

Photography © 2020 Evi Abeler. Food styling by Evi Abeler.
Illustrations used under license from Shutterstock.com.
Author photo courtesy of Shanna Koltz, Koltz Photography.

ISBN: Print 978-1-64739-807-1 | eBook 978-1-64739-482-0
R0

FOR MARK, ALEX, AND GABBY,
WHO BRING SMILES TO MY
FACE AND JOY TO MY HEART
EVERY DAY

CONTENTS

INTRODUCTION

WELCOME TO THE EXCITING WORLD OF COOKING!

My love of cooking goes back to childhood, watching my mom in the kitchen. Mom would make meals from scratch every day, and after school, we were often greeted with her delicious home-made cookies or breads. As I got older, I loved when she would let me make cookies all by myself (although I never liked scooping the cookie dough onto the baking sheet and would ask her to do it for me, which she happily would). Now, I like to cook with my family!

My interest in food and nutrition led me to become a registered dietitian. In fact, I built my business and website, Create Kids Club (CreateKidsClub.com) around my passion for helping kids and adults become confident in the kitchen. I love playing with food and teaching kids (and adults!) how to make healthy cooking simple, tasty, and fun.

When my kids were younger, we spent a lot of time in the kitchen whipping up tasty snacks and treats. Now that they are older, they still enjoy cooking. As you cook your way through this book, I think you'll quickly realize the best part of cooking is sharing the delicious results with the people you love.

I hope this book helps you have fun in your kitchen with your family and friends.

CHAPTER ONE

COOKING BASICS

If you're unsure of where to begin
in the kitchen, I've got you covered.
In this chapter, I'll walk you through common
cooking terms and techniques you'll need to
know to be a successful home cook.

GETTING STARTED

Being comfortable in the kitchen is not only fun, it's also an important skill you will use throughout life. When you know how to cook, a world of possibilities opens up. And cooking doesn't have to be scary. Like all new skills, you'll need to learn the basics before you start. Even the best chefs in the world had to learn these same guidelines when they started.

Before jumping straight into cooking a recipe, read this chapter. It will help you work smart and stay safe in the kitchen so all you'll need to worry about is enjoying the tasty results of your efforts.

A FEW BASIC GUIDELINES

Let's review a few things to keep in mind in the kitchen.

1. **Ask a helper to join you.** Don't worry; many recipes in this book can be completed all on your own. Some, however, do require an adult helper to assist with some tasks. Recipes that need a helper are marked, and your helper can decide if they will complete the task or assist you in doing it.

2. **Read each recipe in full before you start.** Before you begin to prepare any dish, always read the instructions from start to finish—twice. This way, you can organize the ingredients and kitchen tools you'll need before you begin, making sure you have everything.

3. **Set up your workspace.** Find an area in the kitchen where you'll have plenty of space to work. It should be close to everything you need to make the recipe: the oven, micro-wave, and sink. Make sure you can work at a comfortable counter height. Grab a sturdy stool if you need one.

4. **Prepare yourself.** Wash your hands, pull back long hair, roll up loose sleeves, and wear an apron. Aprons not only protect your clothes but also give you something on which to wipe dirty hands. When washing your hands, use plenty of soap and scrub for at least 20 seconds; rinse well.

5. **Wash your food.** Some foods, like fruits and veggies, need to be washed before cutting or eating. Give these items a good rinse under cold running water to remove any visible dirt along with any germs you can't see.

6. **Be safe.** Although working in the kitchen is fun, you always need to be aware of sharp tools, hot surfaces, and food safety. For more details on staying safe, see page 6.

7. **Clean as you go.** Have a dedicated garbage bowl (a medium plastic bowl works great) by your workspace to collect any garbage as well as a clean, damp dishrag to wipe up spills as you go. When you've finished, simply empty the garbage and wipe the counter.

HOW TO FOLLOW A RECIPE

When choosing a recipe to make, consider the time it takes to make the recipe, the steps to complete it (does it need to be cooled or refrigerated before serving?—important when you're looking for a snack right now!), and how many servings it yields (a two-person snack won't be enough to feed four of your friends). The instructions will also tell you if you need to preheat the oven or prep any pans, along with giving you any tips that will help you successfully complete each recipe. For more details on the recipes in this book, turn to page 23.

Labels

Underneath the recipe title you'll find important information about the recipe itself, such as whether it contains nuts or requires a helper.

Prep Time/Cook Time

Each recipe tells you how long, on average, it will take to make. Prep time includes all the steps you need to complete before you start cooking—for example, chopping and mixing. Cook time is the total amount of time needed to cook the food. Your actual times might end up being a little different, and that's okay. These are guidelines to help you when you are planning to cook.

Yield

The "yield" is how much food or how many total servings a recipe makes. It will say something like "Serves 4" or "Makes 24 coins."

Equipment/Ingredients Lists

These lists tell you everything you need to make each recipe, from spatulas to salt. Pro tip: The ingredients are listed in the order you will use them in the recipe.

Instructions

Follow the steps in the order written. Don't forget to read them all from start to finish (twice!) before you start cooking.

Tips/Fun Facts

Some recipes contain additional information that will help you make the recipe and some have fun food facts.

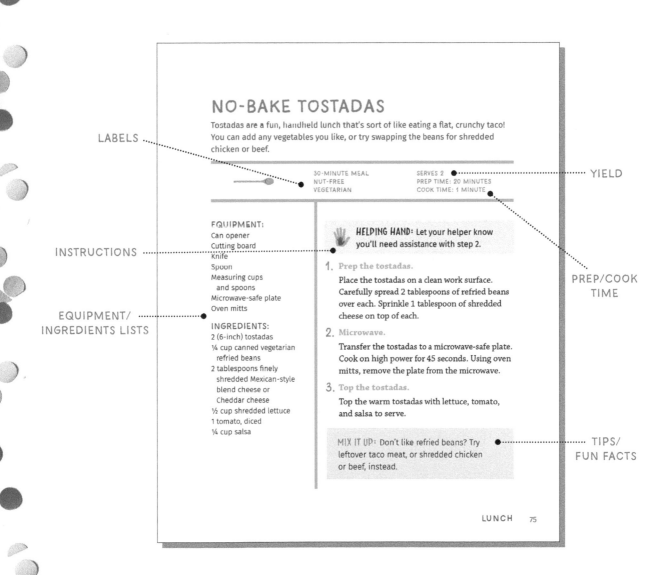

LABELS

INSTRUCTIONS

EQUIPMENT/
INGREDIENTS LISTS

YIELD

PREP/COOK
TIME

TIPS/
FUN FACTS

NO-BAKE TOSTADAS

Tostadas are a fun, handheld lunch that's sort of like eating a flat, crunchy taco! You can add any vegetables you like, or try swapping the beans for shredded chicken or beef.

30-MINUTE MEAL
NUT-FREE
VEGETARIAN

SERVES 2
PREP TIME: 20 MINUTES
COOK TIME: 1 MINUTE

EQUIPMENT:
Can opener
Cutting board
Knife
Spoon
Measuring cups
  and spoons
Microwave-safe plate
Oven mitts

INGREDIENTS:
2 (6-inch) tostadas
¼ cup canned vegetarian
  refried beans
2 tablespoons finely
  shredded Mexican-style
  blend cheese or
  Cheddar cheese
½ cup shredded lettuce
1 tomato, diced
¼ cup salsa

HELPING HAND: Let your helper know you'll need assistance with step 2.

1. **Prep the tostadas.**

   Place the tostadas on a clean work surface. Carefully spread 2 tablespoons of refried beans over each. Sprinkle 1 tablespoon of shredded cheese on top of each.

2. **Microwave.**

   Transfer the tostadas to a microwave-safe plate. Cook on high power for 45 seconds. Using oven mitts, remove the plate from the microwave.

3. **Top the tostadas.**

   Top the warm tostadas with lettuce, tomato, and salsa to serve.

MIX IT UP: Don't like refried beans? Try leftover taco meat, or shredded chicken or beef, instead.

LUNCH   75

ESSENTIAL KITCHEN SAFETY TIPS

1. Wear shoes to help prevent slips and falls and to protect your feet in case you drop something sharp.

2. Never wear loose clothing while cooking—it could accidentally touch the hot stove or get into your food.

3. Ask before you taste test. Some foods, such as chicken, eggs, and fish, need to be cooked before they are safe to eat.

4. Keep temperature-sensitive foods, such as dairy, meat, or seafood, in the refrigerator until you are ready to use them; some foods can spoil if you leave them at room temperature for too long.

5. Never prepare raw meat or fish on the same surface or using the same tools you use to prepare raw fruit or vegetables. You could cross-contaminate them without realizing it and make someone sick.

6. Turn pot handles away from the front of the stove so you don't accidentally bump them or knock them over.

7. Use oven mitts to move hot pots and pans. If the mitts get wet, replace them with dry ones.

8. Be careful when lifting lids off hot food. Always lift lids in the direction opposite you to protect yourself from any hot steam and condensation rising from the hot food.

9. When stirring hot foods, stir away from you to avoid potential splashes.

10. Ask your helper to show you where the fire extinguisher is and how to use it.

TOOLS AND EQUIPMENT

The recipes in this book use common kitchen tools and equipment. If you don't have some of these tools on hand, don't worry. Simply ask your helper what would work as a replacement for that item. As you cook more often, you can work toward getting more tools.

 Baking pan Baking pans come in a variety of shapes and sizes and have sides that are at least 1 or 2 inches tall. They are used in the oven to cook runny batters or thick, solid dishes, such as lasagna.

 Baking sheet/sheet pan A large flat metal baking sheet is used to bake food in the oven. A sheet pan is similar but typically also has short, rimmed sides. A baking sheet does not have any sides.

 Blender A freestanding appliance with a motor base and a blender container used to blend, mix, and puree food.

 **Can opener** Both simple handheld or electric models work equally well for opening cans.

 Colander A bowl, usually metal or plastic, with many holes used to rinse or strain foods.

 Cutting board Plastic or wooden cutting boards protect your work surface and keep knives sharper longer.

Dry measuring cups Dry measuring cups are used to measure dry ingredients such as flour and sugar. They usually come in ¼-, ⅓-, ½-, and 1-cup measures.

 Electric mixer Available as both a handheld tool and a freestanding unit with a bowl. Mixers are used for heavy-duty stirring and combining ingredients. Both models can be set to varying speeds; electric hand mixers typically have two "beaters."

 **Flipper** Also known as a turner or spatula, this tool is used to turn over foods such as burgers, chicken, eggs, and pancakes when cooking. It's also used to serve food. When using a nonstick pan, choose a flexible silicone flipper, as a metal one can scratch the surface.

 Griddle A flat metal cooking surface often used for pancakes or bacon. Available as both freestanding electric units and cast-iron models that sit directly on the stovetop.

 **Knives** A hand tool used for cutting or chopping. You'll need a small chef's knife or nylon knife to chop and cut and a butter knife for spreading things, such as peanut butter.

 Liquid measuring cups Cup with markings on the side of the cup used to measure liquid ingredients, such as oil and milk.

 Measuring spoons Spoons used to measure smaller quantities of ingredients, such as spices and baking powder. Measuring spoons come in varying measures from fractions of a teaspoon to 1 tablespoon.

 Microwave-safe bowls It's very important to use only glass or ceramic bowls in a microwave. Metal bowls will cause electrical problems and plastic bowls can overheat—avoid using them in the microwave.

 Mixing spoons You'll need a few plastic or wooden spoons to combine both dry and wet ingredients (these are larger than the spoons you use to eat).

 Muffin pan A metal or silicone molded pan used to bake muffins or cupcakes in the oven. Available in various sizes—typically 6-, 12-, or 24-cup sizes.

Parchment paper A nonstick baking paper used to line baking pans. Makes removing baked goods and other foods from the pan a snap.

 Pastry bag A cloth or heavy plastic/silicone bag with the end snipped off, used to pipe semisoft foods (like frosting) onto another food or tray in a controlled manner. (You can make your own by snipping off one bottom corner of a sturdy zip-top bag.)

 Pizza cutter Not just for pizza; a pizza cutter is a wheeled cutter that's also great for cutting through quesadillas or flatbread.

 Rubber spatula This is usually referred to simply as a "spatula." It's used to mix food and scrape the sides of a bowl. It's one of the most used kitchen tools. A medium spatula works great.

 Saucepan A deep pan with a handle and a lid used to cook liquids or foods in liquid on the stovetop.

 Skillet A shallow, flat-bottomed pan with slanted sides used to fry, sear, and brown food, usually on the stovetop.

 Stockpot A large, wide-bottomed pan with straight sides, two handles, and a lid, typically used for cooking soups and boiling noodles.

Toaster A small electrical appliance that uses radiant heat to brown bread, making toast. Be careful when removing bread from a toaster: Never insert a fork or other utensil into the toaster.

 Tongs Tongs are helpful for gripping food securely so you can carefully flip or move it. They are great for serving food, too.

 Whisk A whisk is helpful for beating eggs and whipping cream. Whisking is often used in baking to add air into batter.

 Wooden skewers Thin, pointy wooden sticks used to hold foods together, such as for kebabs.

KEEP YOUR INGREDIENTS ON HAND

Having common pantry items on hand gives you the flexibility to cook what you like when the mood strikes, which is why I've included this list of common pantry items you'll need to prepare many of the recipes in this book.

IN THE PANTRY

The following items can be kept at room temperature, in a cupboard or a pantry, until you are ready to use them.

Canned beans Keep a variety on hand, including black beans, chickpeas, pinto beans, and refried beans. Choose low-sodium options when available.

Canned fruits and vegetables Canned fruits and vegetables are a great alternative when fresh are not in season. Stock mandarin oranges, diced tomatoes, and corn kernels. Choose low-sodium, reduced-sugar versions and fruit in natural juices, as they are healthier choices.

Pasta/rice noodles Available in many shapes and sizes. Pasta is typically made from durum wheat. Rice noodles are gluten-free.

Peanut butter/sunflower seed butter Nut butters are a wonderful source of protein. Sunflower seed butter is a great nut-free alternative. I suggest using natural peanut butter. If you do use natural peanut butter, give it a good stir in the jar with a butter knife before using (the oil separates and sits on top).

Pizza sauce/marinara sauce Pizza sauce is used as the red sauce on pizza, whereas marinara is used on spaghetti and other similar dishes. Keep both on hand for the most options.

Precooked rice Precooked rice is sold in microwavable pouches in the rice aisle.

Quick cooking oats Look for "quick cooking" on the package, as this type of oats will cook fast and can be used in baking and sweet treats.

Reduced-sodium chicken or vegetable broth For making everything from soups to sauces, broth is a versatile ingredient. Choose low-sodium options—too much sodium (salt) is not good for our bodies.

Salsa There are many different types of salsa, from sweet to hot. Keep your favorite on hand.

Semisweet chocolate chips Use chips, whole or melted, to make sweet treats. Milk chocolate chips are sweeter and dark chocolate chips are less sweet. Semisweet chocolate chips are a nice balance.

Sugar It's a good idea to limit our sugar intake and a little can go a long way. The different types of sugars found in the recipes include granulated sugar, brown sugar, and powdered sugar.

Whole-wheat tortillas and pitas Use these flatbreads for burritos, sandwiches, and wraps. Choose whole-grain varieties; whole grains are an important part of a healthy diet.

IN THE REFRIGERATOR AND FREEZER

The following items should be kept in your refrigerator or freezer until you are ready to use them.

Cheese Sold shredded or by the block, sharp Cheddar and mozzarella cheeses should be kept in the refrigerator.

Deli meats Sliced turkey and ham can be used in more than just a plain sandwich. Keep a selection in the refrigerator for breakfast, lunch, and dinner.

Eggs Eggs can be baked, fried, poached, or scrambled and play an important role in many recipes. In general, assume large eggs are used unless otherwise specified in a recipe.

Fresh fruits and vegetables Using whatever is in season is a great way to get more fresh fruits and vegetables on your plate. Some great options to have on hand include bananas, blueberries, and grapes along with broccoli, carrots, lettuce, and peppers. Store bananas on the counter—refrigeration turns them brown.

Frozen fruits and vegetables When you can't find fresh foods, frozen is the next best thing. Frozen strawberries and bananas taste fantastic in smoothies. Frozen mixed vegetables are wonderful in stir-fries. Both are quick and easy to use. Keep frozen foods frozen until you're ready to use them.

Milk and heavy (whipping) cream There are many types of milk, including skim, 1 percent, 2 percent, and whole milk, all of which are the same nutritionally except for the amount of fat in them. I tested all these recipes using 1 percent milk. There is also a difference in creams, which are much higher in fat and calories than milk: heavy (whipping) cream, light cream, and half-and-half. I tested most of the recipes using half-and-half (unless heavy cream is specified). If you avoid dairy, some recipes can be altered with nondairy options (like nut- or soy-based products), but the recipes haven't been tested this way.

Plain Greek yogurt and vanilla yogurt Yogurt is very versatile and can be used in baking, cooking, or to eat as-is.

Precooked sausage, sliced pepperoni, frozen meatballs
Precooked sausage, pepperoni, and meatballs can be used in recipes from pizzas to casseroles to reduce cook time. Store them in the same place you find them in the grocery store, either the refrigerator or the freezer.

Premade refrigerated pizza and crescent roll dough Using premade dough cuts prep and cook time and it can be used to make many different kinds of recipes. Keep refrigerated and follow the directions on the package for use.

KEY COOKING SKILLS

You'll notice that the recipes all use common cooking terms and techniques to guide you through preparing each dish. Understanding these terms and techniques can make the difference between delicious results and not-so-tasty ones. You'll practice these skills as you work your way through the recipes in this book.

MEASURING

Measuring ingredients accurately is a very important part of following a recipe. Here are some tips for using measuring cups and spoons.

Measuring Dry Ingredients

To measure dry ingredients, use a spoon to transfer the ingredient to the dry measuring cup. Once the cup is full, use the back (flat side) of a knife to level off the top so you get an exact measure. Do this over a bowl so you can easily pour any excess of the ingredient back into its container. After leveling the ingredient, add it to the recipe as instructed.

Sometimes you'll see measures described as "scant," "rounded," or "heaped." In this book, all measurements are meant to be levelled to the top with a knife, but don't need to be exact.

Sometimes you'll need to use a combination of measuring spoons or measuring cups to get the right amount of an ingredient for your recipe. Most measuring spoon sets come with ¼, ½, and 1 teaspoon and 1 tablespoon. So, if a recipe calls for 1½ teaspoons, you'll add both 1 teaspoon to the bowl along with a ½ teaspoon. Same goes for measuring cups: to get 1¼ cups of flour, use both the 1-cup measure and the ¼-cup measure.

Have questions about the amounts called for in a recipe? Ask your helper for assistance.

Measuring Liquids

When using a liquid measuring cup, bend down so you are at eye level with the measuring marks on the cup (otherwise you may pour in too much or too little). Sometimes a recipe will call for more liquid than your measuring cup allows for. If you have a 1-cup measuring cup and the recipe calls for 2 cups of something, pour the first cup, then measure the second cup.

USING SHARP TOOLS

Learning how to use a knife properly, as well as safely, will help you chop like a pro and prevent cuts. You'll only need one knife for the recipes in this book: a nylon knife or a small chef's knife. The following knife skills apply to chefs of all levels—from beginner to advanced. My kids used nylon knives until they not only understood how to properly hold and cut with a knife but also were able to use their skills consistently. Your adult helper can decide which knife you should start with.

How to Cut and Chop

It's important to be at the correct height in relation to the counter when chopping: Your waist should be even with or just below the counter. Stand on a sturdy step stool if you need a boost up.

Next, you'll need a cutting board. To keep the cutting board in place, put a damp kitchen towel underneath (but make sure your cutting board sits evenly on top of it).

To get started, grip the handle of the knife with your writing hand. Hold the knife with a bicycle grip (how your hands look if holding handlebars). Your knuckles should be facing up. Place your thumb and pointer finger where the blade of the knife and the handle meet, then wrap your fingers around the handle. Do not place your pointer finger on the top of the blade.

Place the item you are cutting on the board so it lays flat. In the case of something round, it's safer to cut it in half lengthwise, lay the item flat-side down, then work with only one half at a time. Then, using your other hand, hold the item in place, curling your fingers under like a claw, making sure to tuck your thumb in. By curling your fingers under, you protect them in case the knife slips. If your knife slips, the flat side will knock your knuckles instead of cutting your fingers.

When cutting, it helps to pretend the tip of the knife is stuck to the cutting board and move the blade in a rocking motion, instead of picking the blade up off the board every time you make a cut. Use your knife to cut, not saw, through the food.

To cut, slowly push the food toward the knife.

To coarsely chop or cut small pieces, place your hand flat on top of the knife, pushing down, as you rock the knife across the food.

OTHER SHARP TOOLS

When working in the kitchen you'll use other sharp tools as well.

Apple corer Place the apple corer on the stem side (top) of the apple. Holding the handles of the tool, carefully push it down, keeping your fingers away from the blades.

Box grater/zester A box grater has four sides that grate, shred, and slice. A zester is a long, flat tool with small holes that shave more finely and consistently than a box grater. When using either tool, hold the handle, keep your fingers away from the cutting surface, and push the food away from your body. Ask a helper to assist you, if needed.

Peelers Hold the peeler in your writing hand. Peel away from your body.

USING THE STOVE

To use an electric stove:

- Place the pan on a burner.
- Find the knob that controls the burner your pan is sitting on. There may be a diagram on the knob or on the stove.
- Turn the knob to the setting indicated in the recipe.
- When you are done cooking, turn off the burner before removing the pan. Be careful; the burner will remain hot.

To use a gas stove:

- Place the pan on a burner.
- Find the knob that controls the burner your pan is sitting on. There may be a diagram on the knob or on the stove.
- To ignite the flames, push in the knob until you hear a clicking sound and then quickly turn the knob to the heat setting

indicated in the recipe. The clicking sound is made by the ignitor, which makes the spark to create the flame. If you don't see a flame immediately, quickly turn off the knob and try again.

- When you are done cooking, turn off the burner before removing the pan. Be careful; the burner will remain hot.

With both types of stoves, ask a helper to assist you, if needed.

USING THE OVEN

Ovens work by heating air, which, in turn, cooks the food. Always check that the oven is empty before turning it on. Here are a few other things to keep in mind.

- Pay attention to which oven rack the recipe instructs you to use. Although most recipes are cooked on the middle rack, it can vary. If a recipe doesn't specify a rack, you can assume that using the middle oven rack is fine. You want to adjust the oven rack's position while the oven is cold.
- Before placing food in the oven, it's important that the oven is at the proper cooking temperature, so you'll need to turn on the oven before you need it; this is called **preheating**, and it usually takes about 10 minutes for an oven to get up to heat, though it might be longer or shorter depending on your oven. Preheat the oven to the temperature directed in the recipe.
- Make sure to set the oven timer according to the cook time indicated in the recipe so your food isn't burned or undercooked.
- Always use dry oven mitts when removing food from the oven. The water in a damp oven mitt will become steam when you touch something hot, and can cause burns. Ask a helper to assist you, if needed.

OTHER IMPORTANT SKILLS

Blending Using an electric blender is the best way to mix two soft ingredients to a smooth consistency. While it is unplugged, assemble the blender by placing the blender jar onto the motor base, if needed. Plug in the blender. Make sure the lid is secure before turning on the blender or you may end up with a real mess.

Combining Always add ingredients to a bowl in the order instructed. Unless the recipe says otherwise, use a spoon or spatula to mix them.

Creaming Blending a solid fat, such as butter, until it's smooth, then mixing it with other ingredients, such as sugar. This technique is often used in making cookie doughs and cake batters.

Dicing round foods Carefully cut off the stem of the food you're dicing, then cut the item in half. Place the cut halves, cut-side down, onto your cutting board. Using a knife, cut the food both horizontally and vertically into small bite-size pieces.

Folding When you need to combine two different ingredients but keep air in the mixture, you "fold" one ingredient into the other. You do this using a wooden spoon or spatula, turning the ingredients over each other just until they are incorporated.

Greasing Use a nonstick cooking spray to coat the bottom and sides of your pan lightly before filling it with food. This prevents the food from sticking to the pan when cooking.

Juicing Some recipes call for the fresh juice of a lemon, lime, or other citrus fruit. It's easy to juice citrus using a manual juicer. Place half a lemon or lime, flesh-side down, on the top of the juicer. Twist the fruit until no more juice comes out.

Mixing Use an electric beater or stand mixer to combine or whip ingredients thoroughly. To use an electric beater, while the machine is unplugged, place the beater(s) into the slots in the mixer. Plug in the mixer. Place the beaters into the mixing bowl and then turn it on low speed. Always start on low and gradually increase the speed as directed in the recipe. To use a stand mixer, use the paddle or beater attachment as directed, and make sure the bowl and the top of the mixer are locked into place before starting.

Shaving Parmesan cheese Use a vegetable peeler (peeling away from your body) to shave a block of Parmesan cheese into thin strips (rather than using a box grater to finely grate the cheese).

Shredding When shredding foods, use your hands to break the food item into smaller pieces, such as tearing lettuce into bite-sized piece or pulling cooked chicken apart into smaller, easier-to-eat portions.

Simmering/boiling When cooking liquids, you'll be asked to heat them to either a simmer or a boil. To simmer means heating a liquid until small bubbles form on top. Boiling requires a hotter heat. A food boils when large bubbles vigorously appear on top.

Testing food temperature When preparing some foods, especially meat and fish, it's important to cook them until they reach a temperature safe for consumption. You can check the temperature of food by using a cooking thermometer. To use, push the thermometer about one-third of the way into the thickest part of the food. If it reads below the recommended temperature, continue cooking the food and check again. Ask a helper to assist you, if needed.

FREQUENTLY ASKED QUESTIONS

WHY DO I NEED A HELPER?

This book is for beginners and safety is important. As you become comfortable in the kitchen, your helper can decide when you can safely do more on your own.

WHY DO I NEED TO WASH MY HANDS SO MUCH?

Proper handwashing prevents foodborne illness. When switching from raw foods like meat to fresh foods like vegetables, it's important to wash your hands to prevent cross-contamination. Heating foods to proper temperatures kills germs, but food that's not cooked can be full of germs that were passed along from dirty hands.

I DON'T HAVE AN INGREDIENT. WHAT SHOULD I DO?

If you're missing a fruit or vegetable, simply swap it out for another similar fruit or veggie you have at home. You can swap things like flour tortillas for corn tortillas or flatbreads. If you don't have chicken, but have beef or pork, use that instead.

MY FINISHED DISH DOESN'T TASTE GOOD. WHAT HAPPENED?

Reread the recipe to see if you skipped a step or ingredient. Some recipes can be fixed by adjusting the seasonings. If you added too much seasoning, you can add more of another ingredient. For example, if you added too much vanilla extract to a yogurt dip, add more yogurt to cut down on the vanilla flavor.

WHICH RECIPE SHOULD I START WITH?

All the recipes in this book are meant for beginning cooks. Each recipe is rated 1, 2, or 3 spoons: 1 spoon is the easiest, so I recommend starting with one of these recipes.

ABOUT THE RECIPES

Every recipe found in this book is designed for beginning cooks using common ingredients, including fresh, canned, and frozen items.

If it's your first time in the kitchen, try the Oatmeal Peanut Butter Balls (page 57). If you're looking for a tasty treat and are willing to wait a little to eat it, I highly recommend the Frozen S'mores (page 127). If you're planning to cook dinner for your family for the first time, be sure to try the Cheeseburger Sliders (page 92).

LABELS

Each recipe includes a label or two under the title to give you extra insight into each dish. If you want to choose a recipe based on these qualifications, check out the Label Index on page 146. Here's a key:

5 Ingredients or Less These recipes can be made using 5 ingredients or fewer.

10 Minutes or Less These recipes can be made, from start to finish, in 10 minutes or less.

30-Minute Meal These recipes can be made, from start to finish, in 30 minutes.

No Help Needed These recipes can be made on your own with no assistance from your adult helper.

Nut-Free These recipes do not contain products containing nuts.

Vegetarian These recipes do not contain meat.

DIFFICULTY SCALE

Each recipe includes a difficulty rating. If you want to choose a recipe based on how challenging it is, check out the Difficulty Index on page 145.

——● 1 wooden spoon = Easiest
Basic recipes perfect for absolute beginners. These, generally, are made with the fewest ingredients and number of steps to follow.

——● 2 wooden spoons = Easier
A step up from Easiest to learn new skills. You will use more ingredients and have additional steps to follow.

——● 3 wooden spoons = Easy
Still simple to prepare but these recipes use more cooking skills. These recipes build on the skills learned in easier recipes and have the most steps to follow.

TIPS

You will find three types of cooking tips at the end of many recipes:

Mix It Up These tips suggest ingredient swaps.

Getting Messy These tips suggest ways to make the recipe turn out great.

Fun Facts These tips provide interesting information about food.

Rainbow Smoothie Bowl,
page 28

CHAPTER TWO
BREAKFAST

RAINBOW SMOOTHIE BOWL

This blueberry-banana smoothie bowl is blended together, then served with a fruit rainbow. My daughter likes to swap the blueberries for strawberries to create a whole new flavor. If you're not ready to try spinach in your smoothie, simply omit it. You'll only need a small handful of each type of fruit for topping.

30-MINUTE MEAL
NUT-FREE
VEGETARIAN

SERVES 2
PREP TIME: 20 MINUTES

EQUIPMENT:
Can opener
Blender
Measuring cups
  and spoons
Serving spoon
2 serving bowls

INGREDIENTS:
½ overripe banana
1 (11-ounce) can mandarin
  oranges in juice, or 1 fresh
  tangerine or clementine
½ cup pineapple chunks
  (canned in juice, or fresh)
1 cup fresh raspberries
½ cup green
  seedless grapes
¼ cup fresh blueberries
1 cup fresh spinach
⅔ cup frozen blueberries
½ cup milk
2 teaspoons honey

HELPING HAND: Let your helper know you'll need assistance with steps 1, 2, and 3.

1. **Prepare the fruit.**

   Peel the banana and break it in half. (Eat the other half, or place it into a resealable bag and refrigerate or freeze it for later.) Open the cans of mandarin oranges and pineapple and drain them. Rinse the raspberries, grapes, and fresh blueberries. Cut the grapes in half.

2. **Put the ingredients into the blender.**

   In a blender, combine the spinach, frozen blueberries, banana, milk, and honey.

3. **Puree the mixture.**

   Secure the lid onto the blender and puree the mixture until it's smooth.

4. **Portion the bowls.**

   Divide the smoothie evenly between two shallow bowls.

5. **Decorate!**

Arrange the fruit on the puree in a rainbow pattern: Working from left to right, I like raspberries, oranges, pineapple, grapes, and blueberries. Check out the picture on page 26 for inspiration!

I HEART STRAWBERRIES PARFAIT

Vanilla yogurt is topped with heart-shaped strawberries and granola or dry cereal for a quick and tasty treat. Get creative with the toppings: Add extra fruit or mix your favorite cereals. This recipe is fun to make with friends.

5 INGREDIENTS OR LESS
10 MINUTES OR LESS
NO HELP NEEDED
VEGETARIAN

SERVES 1
PREP TIME: 10 MINUTES

EQUIPMENT:
Spoon
Parfait cup or regular
  drinking glass
Cutting board
Knife
Measuring cups
  and spoons

INGREDIENTS:
½ cup vanilla yogurt
2 to 4 fresh strawberries,
  rinsed and dried
1 to 2 tablespoons granola
  or dry cereal
Heart-shaped sprinkles
  (optional)

1. **Scoop the yogurt.**

   Put the yogurt into a parfait cup or short, widemouthed glass.

2. **Cut the strawberries.**

   Put the strawberries onto a cutting board. Position a strawberry on its side and cut a V-shape into the top of the strawberry to cut out the stem. Halve the strawberry lengthwise so it looks like a little heart.

3. **Assemble the parfaits.**

   Arrange the strawberries on top of the yogurt. Sprinkle with granola and decorate with sprinkles (if using).

   MIX IT UP: Use different yogurt flavors for a fun twist. Use small, heart-shaped cookie cutters on sliced watermelon, cantaloupe, or pineapple for a variety of fruit hearts.

PEANUT BUTTER BANANA WAFFLEWICH

Peanut butter and honey sandwiches were a childhood favorite of mine—my mom sent them in my school lunchbox every day. I combined that memory with my kids' favorite—waffles—to come up with this yummy and filling breakfast sandwich.

5 INGREDIENTS OR LESS
10 MINUTES OR LESS
VEGETARIAN

SERVES 1
PREP TIME: 10 MINUTES
COOK TIME: 2 MINUTES

EQUIPMENT:
Toaster
Butter knife
Cutting board
Measuring spoons

INGREDIENTS:
2 frozen
    whole-grain waffles
1 small banana
1 to 2 tablespoons
    smooth peanut butter or
    sunflower seed butter
Honey, for drizzling

 HELPING HAND: Have your helper assist you with step 1 when removing the waffles from the toaster.

1. **Prepare the waffles.**

   Put the waffles into a toaster. Toast for about 1½ minutes until lightly browned.

2. **Cut the fruit.**

   Peel the banana, then place it onto your cutting board and cut it into bite-size pieces.

3. **Assemble the sandwich.**

   Spread the peanut butter onto one of the toasted waffles. Arrange the banana pieces on top of the peanut butter. Drizzle with honey, then cover with the other waffle to make a sandwich.

MIX IT UP: Try strawberries and chocolate-hazelnut spread, or cream cheese with raspberries, for a whole new version.

FUN FACT: Honey is the only food you can eat straight that will never go bad. It keeps forever!

BREAKFAST BURRITO

This quick and tasty breakfast can be made the night before and reheated in the microwave when you're ready to eat. I like to keep these in my freezer for last-minute meals.

5 INGREDIENTS OR LESS
30-MINUTE MEAL
NUT-FREE

SERVES 1
PREP TIME: 10 MINUTES
COOK TIME:
1 MINUTE 25 SECONDS

EQUIPMENT:
Microwave-safe bowl
  and plate
Fork
Measuring cups
  and spoons

INGREDIENTS:
2 large eggs
Salt
Freshly ground
  black pepper
1 large (10-inch)
  whole-wheat flour tortilla
¼ cup precooked turkey
  sausage crumbles
1 to 2 tablespoons frozen
  diced bell pepper, thawed
1 tablespoon shredded
  cheese (Cheddar or
  mozzarella work well)

 HELPING HAND: Let your helper know you'll need assistance with step 1, scrambling the eggs.

1. **Make the eggs.**

   Following the recipe for Quick and Easy Scrambled Eggs (page 39), cook the eggs.

2. **Fill the burrito.**

   Place the tortilla on a clean work surface. Arrange the turkey sausage, bell pepper, scrambled eggs, and cheese on top.

3. **Fold the tortilla.**

   To wrap into a burrito, fold the sides of the tortilla in toward the middle of the burrito, then carefully fold the bottom of the burrito around the eggs and meat, pulling gently toward you to create a tight roll, then roll up the rest of the way.

4. **Heat the burrito.**

Place the burrito on a microwave-safe plate and microwave on high power for 25 seconds.

MIX IT UP: Add some fresh spinach leaves or diced tomato to the burrito before wrapping for an extra boost of veggies!

FUN FACT: Eggs are a food rich in iron. Did you know your body contains enough iron to make a 1-inch-long nail? You even contain a little bit of gold!

PUMPKIN PANCAKES

Pancakes make a weekly appearance in my home. This recipe has been modified many times over the years. I started by adding applesauce to the batter to make the pancakes extra moist, then experimented with other fruit purees, eventually ending with this delicious pumpkin version.

30-MINUTE MEAL
VEGETARIAN

MAKES 14 PANCAKES
PREP TIME: 10 MINUTES
COOK TIME:
4 MINUTES PER BATCH

EQUIPMENT:
Measuring cups
  and spoons
2 medium bowls
Whisk
Wooden spoon
Griddle or large skillet
Can opener
Flipper

INGREDIENTS:
1½ cups all-purpose flour
1½ teaspoons
  baking powder
1 teaspoon baking soda
1 teaspoon pumpkin
  pie spice
1 teaspoon ground
  cinnamon
½ teaspoon salt
1½ cups milk
½ cup canned pure
  pumpkin puree

 HELPING HAND: Let your helper know you'll need assistance with steps 4 and 5.

1. **Combine the dry ingredients.**

   In a medium bowl, whisk the flour, baking powder, baking soda, pumpkin pie spice, cinnamon, and salt to blend. Set aside.

2. **Combine the wet ingredients.**

   In another medium bowl, whisk the milk, pumpkin, egg, oil, brown sugar, and almond extract until combined.

3. **Fold them together.**

   Add the wet ingredients to the dry ingredients. Using a wooden spoon, stir just until moistened. It's okay if there are some lumps. Don't overmix the batter because this will make your pancakes tough.

   continued >>

1 large egg
2 tablespoons vegetable oil
2 tablespoons light
 brown sugar
1 teaspoon almond extract
 or vanilla extract
1 tablespoon butter, plus
 more as needed
Prepared fruit, for serving
Warmed maple syrup,
 for serving

4. **Preheat the griddle.**

Preheat the griddle to 350°F, or heat a large nonstick skillet over medium heat. Melt the butter in the pan.

5. **Cook the pancakes.**

Working in batches, using a ¼-cup measuring cup, scoop pancake batter and pour it onto the hot griddle or skillet (don't crowd the pancakes or they will be hard to flip). Cook the pancakes for 1½ to 2 minutes per side. You'll know it's time to flip the pancakes when the edges start to get a little browned and the center of the pancake batter is bubbly. As the pancakes are finished, use the flipper to move them to a plate and cover it with aluminum foil to keep them warm. Repeat with the remaining batter, adding more butter to the skillet if your pancakes start to stick. Serve with fruit and syrup.

MIX IT UP: Add a handful of semisweet chocolate chips to the dry ingredients in step 1 if you'd like your pancakes a little sweeter.

QUICK AND EASY SCRAMBLED EGGS

Do you know you can cook eggs in the microwave in just 1 minute? Add veggies, ham, or cheese to make an "omelet"—just make sure you use a deep enough microwave-safe bowl so your eggs don't spill over.

5 INGREDIENTS OR LESS
10 MINUTES OR LESS
NUT-FREE

SERVES 1
PREP TIME: 5 MINUTES
COOK TIME: 1 MINUTE

EQUIPMENT:
Small microwave-safe bowl
Fork
Spoon

INGREDIENTS:
2 large eggs
Salt
Freshly ground
   black pepper

MIX IT UP: Add finely chopped green bell pepper, diced tomato, or shredded cheese in step 2, before cooking.

 HELPING HAND: Let your helper know you'll need assistance with steps 1 and 3.

1. **Crack the eggs.**

   Crack the eggs into a small, microwave-safe bowl. Season with a sprinkle of salt and pepper.

2. **Whisk the eggs.**

   Using a fork, whisk the eggs until they're uniform in color, with no visible streaks of the white.

3. **Cook the eggs.**

   Place the bowl of eggs into the microwave. Microwave on high power for 1 minute. Using a clean spoon, "scramble" or break apart the eggs. If the eggs still have some liquid, continue to cook them in 10-second increments, taking care not to overcook them. The eggs will continue to cook a little more after you remove them from the microwave.

GLAZED FRENCH TOAST MUFFINS

These muffins are a no-fail version of French toast and are baked in the oven rather than cooked on the stovetop. Using cinnamon-raisin bread and a sweet glaze elevates this French toast above the rest.

30-MINUTE MEAL
NUT-FREE
VEGETARIAN

SERVES 6
PREP TIME: 15 MINUTES
COOK TIME: 15 MINUTES

EQUIPMENT:
6-cup muffin pan
Paper muffin liners
  (optional)
Bowls: medium and small
Measuring cups
  and spoons
Large spoon
Cutting board
Knife
Oven mitts

INGREDIENTS:
Nonstick cooking spray
2 large eggs
2 tablespoons plus
  1 teaspoon milk, divided
1 tablespoon
  granulated sugar
½ teaspoon ground
  cinnamon
½ teaspoon vanilla extract
4 slices
  cinnamon-raisin bread
¼ cup powdered sugar

 HELPING HAND: Ask your helper to assist you with step 6, placing the muffins into the oven and removing them once cooked.

1. **Preheat the oven to 350°F.**

   Generously coat a 6-cup muffin pan with cooking spray, or line it with paper liners.

2. **Prepare the egg mixture.**

   Crack the eggs into a medium bowl. Add 2 tablespoons of milk, the granulated sugar, cinnamon, and vanilla. Stir well to blend.

3. **Cut the bread.**

   Place the bread slices on a cutting board and cut each into thirds, both horizontally and vertically, to make bread cubes, or tear the bread into bite-size chunks.

4. **Combine the egg mixture and bread.**

   Stir the bread cubes into the egg mixture, taking care to coat all the bread.

continued >>

5. **Place the bread mixture in the pan.**

Evenly divide the bread cube mixture among the prepared muffin cups. Gently press the bread down with the back of a spoon.

6. **Bake.**

Transfer the pan to the preheated oven and bake for 15 minutes, or until golden brown. Using oven mitts, remove the pan from the oven.

7. **Glaze the muffins.**

Meanwhile, in a small bowl, stir together the powdered sugar and the remaining 1 teaspoon of milk. Pour the glaze over the warm muffins in the muffin pan.

8. **Serve.**

French toast muffins are best enjoyed warm. To reheat, simply microwave them on high power for 45 seconds, or until warmed.

MIX IT UP: For a different spin on this recipe, use cranberry-orange bread, banana bread, or other flavored breads. Add a handful of peeled, chopped apple, nuts, or dried fruit in step 4.

AMAZING OVERNIGHT OATS

It's pretty fun waking up knowing you have a special breakfast in the fridge. This oatmeal is prepared in advance and placed in the refrigerator overnight so it's ready for breakfast when you are. Because the oats soak up the milk, they have a creamy texture.

5 INGREDIENTS OR LESS
NO HELP NEEDED
VEGETARIAN

SERVES 1
PREP TIME: 10 MINUTES, PLUS
OVERNIGHT TO SOAK

EQUIPMENT:
Resealable container
  with lid
Measuring cups
  and spoons
Spoon

INGREDIENTS:
½ cup quick cooking oats
¾ cup milk
1 tablespoon unsweetened
  dried fruit, such as
  raisins, cranberries,
  blueberries, etc.
1 tablespoon sweetened
  shredded coconut

1. **Combine.**

   In a small Mason jar or other sealable container, stir together the oats, milk, dried fruit, and coconut until well combined.

2. **Refrigerate.**

   Cover the jar and place it into the refrigerator overnight, or for at least 2 hours.

GETTING MESSY: You can also make overnight oats in the morning for an afternoon snack. If you don't feel like waiting, these oats can be eaten right away. (That's actually the way my kids prefer to eat them.)

MIX IT UP: Add fresh fruit before serving. Drizzle with honey for extra sweetness.

Strawberry Fruit Leather,
page 48

CHAPTER THREE
SNACKS

POPCORN SEASONING TWO WAYS

Spice up your next movie night with some zesty popcorn. Cheesy Ranch Seasoning and Salted Caramel Seasoning are easy to make and take popcorn to the next level. To get seasonings to stick better to the popcorn, lightly spray the popcorn with cooking spray before adding the seasonings.

5 INGREDIENTS OR LESS
10 MINUTES OR LESS
NO HELP NEEDED
NUT-FREE
VEGETARIAN

MAKES ABOUT ½ CUP
PREP TIME: 10 MINUTES

EQUIPMENT:

Measuring spoons
Small bowl
Blender or spice grinder
Spoon
Resealable bag or empty
   saltshaker

INGREDIENTS:

FOR THE CHEESY RANCH
SEASONING

3 tablespoons
   garlic powder
2 tablespoons
   powdered cheese
1 tablespoon salt
2½ teaspoons
   onion powder
2 teaspoons dried dill

1. **To make the cheesy ranch seasoning:** In a small bowl, stir together the garlic powder, powdered cheese, salt, onion powder, and dill until well combined.

   To make the salted caramel seasoning: In a blender or clean spice grinder, combine the turbinado sugar, brown sugar, powdered sugar, and salt. Blend until well combined.

2. **Store the seasoning.**

   Transfer the mixture to a resealable bag or clean saltshaker. Both seasonings will keep at room temperature for up to 1 month.

3. **Serve over popcorn.**

   Mist the popped popcorn with cooking spray (or toss with melted butter) and sprinkle or shake on about 1 teaspoon of seasoning for every 2 cups of popped popcorn.

FOR THE SALTED CARAMEL
SEASONING

3 tablespoons
   turbinado sugar
2½ tablespoons light
   brown sugar
2 tablespoons
   powdered sugar
1 teaspoon salt

FOR SERVING:

Plain popped popcorn
   (see Getting Messy)
Nonstick cooking spray or
   melted butter

GETTING MESSY: You don't have to buy bags of microwave popcorn, because it's easy (and cheap) to do it yourself: Place ¼ cup of popcorn kernels in a brown paper lunch bag. Fold over the top to seal the bag and put the bag in the microwave. Cook on high power for 2 to 3 minutes. Stop the microwave when the popping slows and be careful of escaping steam when you open the bag. This will make about 7 cups of popcorn.

STRAWBERRY FRUIT LEATHER

Fruit Roll-Up lookalikes are easy to make at home—they just take a little time to dry in the oven. You can have fun with the shape, too: Cut this fruit leather into strips or use your favorite cookie cutters.

5 INGREDIENTS OR LESS
NUT-FREE
VEGETARIAN

SERVES 4
PREP TIME: 20 MINUTES
COOK TIME: 6 TO 8 HOURS

EQUIPMENT:
Measuring cups
Baking sheets (2)
Parchment paper or
   silicone mat liner
Cutting board
Knife
Blender or food processor
Pizza cutter
Flipper

INGREDIENTS:
7 cups fresh strawberries

 HELPING HAND: Let your helper know you'll need assistance with step 4.

1. **Preheat the oven to the lowest setting, 150°F to 170°F.**

   Line 2 baking sheets with parchment paper or silicone mat liners.

2. **Prep the strawberries.**

   Place the strawberries onto a cutting board. Position a strawberry on its side and cut a V-shape into the top of the strawberry to cut out the stem. Repeat with all the strawberries.

3. **Blend the strawberries.**

   Transfer the fruit to a blender or food processor. Cover with the lid and blend until the fruit is pureed. Divide the pureed fruit between the prepared baking sheets.

4. **Bake the fruit leather.**

   Place the baking sheets in the oven and bake for 6 to 8 hours, or until the middle is set and looks dry. Remove from the oven and let cool completely.

5. **Slice.**

   Using a pizza cutter, cut the cooled leather into strips or use cookie cutters to cut out fun shapes.

MIX IT UP: Swap strawberries for your favorite fruit or use a combination of fruits. This recipe works well with frozen fruit, too—thaw and drain it before you use it (check the package for thawing instructions).

LEMON-LIME SODA

Who doesn't like lemon-lime soda? This version is low in sugar, making it much better for you than store-bought varieties. Customize your soda using different fruit juices. You can also add smashed strawberries, raspberries, blueberries, or other fruit for a boost of flavor.

5 INGREDIENTS OR LESS
10 MINUTES OR LESS
NO HELP NEEDED
NUT-FREE
VEGETARIAN

SERVES 2
PREP TIME: 10 MINUTES

EQUIPMENT:
Knife
Small bowl
Juicer (optional)
Measuring cups
    and spoons
2 tall glasses

INGREDIENTS:
1 lemon, halved
1 lime, halved
¼ cup frozen apple juice
    concentrate, thawed, or
    more to taste
Ice cubes, for serving
1¼ cups sparkling water

1. **Juice the citrus fruit.**

   Squeeze the juice from the lemon and lime halves into a small bowl, or use a juicer.

2. **Combine the ingredients.**

   In a drinking glass, stir together 3 tablespoons of freshly squeezed citrus juice and 2 tablespoons of apple juice concentrate. Repeat in the other glass.

3. **Finish the drinks.**

   Add ice to each glass and top with sparkling water. Stir.

   GETTING MESSY: Apple juice concentrate is found in the freezer section of your grocery store. Save the extra in a resealable bag or make a pitcher of apple juice following the directions on the can.

MANDARIN ORANGE FRUIT DIP

This delicious fruit dip is perfect for a snack or for packing with your lunch. Although you can dip away with your favorite fruit or crackers (think apple slices, strawberries, graham crackers, or animal crackers), consider switching things up and trying something you don't like quite as much. I'm betting you'll find this dip makes it much more enjoyable!

5 INGREDIENTS OR LESS
10 MINUTES OR LESS
NO HELP NEEDED
NUT-FREE
VEGETARIAN

SERVES 6 TO 8
PREP TIME: 10 MINUTES

EQUIPMENT:
Medium bowl
Measuring cups
  and spoons
Can opener
Handheld electric mixer
Spatula

INGREDIENTS:
1 cup low-fat vanilla yogurt
  (Greek yogurt works great)
½ cup cream cheese
  (half of an 8-ounce
  package), at room
  temperature
1 (11-ounce) can mandarin
  oranges in light
  syrup, drained
1 teaspoon vanilla extract
Sliced apples and
  strawberries or graham
  crackers, for serving

1. **Combine the dip ingredients.**

   In a medium bowl, combine the yogurt, cream cheese, mandarin oranges, and vanilla.

2. **Blend the dip.**

   Using a hand mixer, blend the ingredients on low speed until the cream cheese is well incorporated. Stop and use a spatula to scrape down the sides of the bowl, as needed.

3. **Serve the dip.**

   Using the spatula, scrape the dip into a serving bowl and serve with your dippers of choice.

MIX IT UP: To bring the cream cheese to room temperature, set it on the counter 30 minutes to 1 hour ahead of time. This softens the cream cheese so it's easier to blend into other foods.

FUN FACT: Did you know there are "fruit salad trees" that can produce up to six different kinds of fruit all on one tree? Producers graft together fruit trees from the same family onto one tree.

FRUIT SALSA

Did you know you can make salsa with fruit? This sweet and tangy version blends a variety of fruits with lemon and lime juice and adds extra sweetness with jelly. You can swap out fruits for those you have on hand and use any kind of jelly or jam you like best. Serve with Cinnamon Sugar Chips (page 60) for a sweet and crunchy snack or appetizer!

30-MINUTE MEAL
NUT-FREE
VEGETARIAN

SERVES 4 TO 6
PREP TIME: 20 MINUTES

EQUIPMENT:
Cutting board
Knife
Apple corer
Bowls: medium and small
Juicer
Measuring cups
   and spoons
Wooden spoon

INGREDIENTS:
1 pint fresh strawberries
1 apple
5 to 10 seedless green or
   purple grapes
1 pint fresh blueberries
1 pint fresh raspberries
1 tablespoon freshly
   squeezed lemon juice
   (from about ½ lemon)
1 tablespoon freshly
   squeeze lime juice (from
   about ½ lime)

 HELPING HAND: Let your helper know you'll need assistance chopping the fruit in step 1.

1. **Prepare the fruit.**

   Cut the stems out of the strawberries and chop the strawberries. Use an apple corer to remove the core of the apple and chop the apple. Cut the grapes into halves. Put the chopped strawberries and apple and the grape halves into a medium bowl. Add the blueberries and raspberries.

2. **Prepare the dressing.**

   In a small bowl, stir together the lemon juice, lime juice, and jelly until blended. Pour the dressing over the fruit and gently stir to coat the fruit pieces with the dressing.

continued >>

2 to 3 tablespoons
   raspberry jelly
Cinnamon Sugar Chips
   (page 60) or sweet pita
   chips (such as Stacy's
   Cinnamon Sugar Pita
   Chips), for serving

3. **Serve.**

Serve with cinnamon sugar chips for dipping.

MIX IT UP: If you like spicy salsa, add 1 to
2 tablespoons diced jalapeño pepper (ask a
helper for assistance chopping the jalapeño,
as their oils can burn). Serve with regular
tortilla or pita chips.

OATMEAL PEANUT BUTTER BALLS

This sweet treat doesn't last long at my house, and I bet it won't at yours, either. To make it easier to get the honey out of the measuring cup, spray the cup with cooking spray before measuring the honey.

5 INGREDIENTS OR LESS
10 MINUTES OR LESS
NO HELP NEEDED
VEGETARIAN

MAKES ABOUT 24 BALLS
PREP TIME: 20 MINUTES

EQUIPMENT:
Measuring cups
  and spoons
Medium bowl
Wooden spoon
Plate
Plastic wrap

INGREDIENTS:
2 cups quick cooking oats
½ cup honey
½ cup smooth
  peanut butter
1 teaspoon vanilla extract

FUN FACT: Oatmeal cookies are the number-one use for oatmeal (besides eating it as a cereal), followed by meatloaf.

1. **Combine the ingredients.**

   In a medium bowl, stir together the oats, honey, peanut butter, and vanilla until combined.

2. **Shape the balls.**

   Using clean hands, roll about 2 tablespoons of the batter into a ball and place it on a plate. Repeat with the remaining batter. You should get about 24 balls.

3. **Store the balls.**

   Cover the balls with plastic wrap and refrigerate for up to 1 week.

MIX IT UP: Add ½ cup semisweet chocolate chips, sweetened dried cranberries, or your favorite chopped nuts in step 1.

TACO HUMMUS

My favorite way to eat fresh veggies is to dip them into hummus. Hummus is a bean-based dip that can be made fresh at home very easily. It's versatile, too—instead of adding taco seasoning, as here, try dry ranch seasoning or sriracha.

10 MINUTES OR LESS
NO HELP NEEDED
NUT-FREE
VEGETARIAN

SERVES 4
PREP TIME: 15 MINUTES

EQUIPMENT:
Can opener
Knife
Juicer
Blender or food processor
Measuring spoons
Spatula
Serving dish

INGREDIENTS:
2 (15-ounce) cans
   low-sodium chickpeas,
   drained (reserve ½ cup of
   liquid from one can)
1 (1-ounce) packet
   low-sodium taco
   seasoning
Juice of ½ lemon
2 tablespoons tahini
Cut fresh veggies, Tortilla
   Chips (page 60), or
   whole-grain crackers,
   for serving

1. **Combine the blender.**

In a blender or food processor, combine the chickpeas, taco seasoning, lemon juice, tahini, and 1 tablespoon of reserved liquid from the can. Put the lid on the blender and blend until smooth. If the hummus is too thick, add more reserved liquid from the can, 1 tablespoon at a time, to help the ingredients blend to the desired consistency.

2. **Garnish.**

Using a spatula, transfer the hummus to a serving dish. Serve with veggies, tortilla chips, or whole-grain crackers for dipping.

FUN FACT: The liquid in the can of chickpeas is called aquafaba. It's the water the beans have been cooked in. This liquid can be used to replace eggs in recipes such as marshmallows.

TORTILLA OR CINNAMON SUGAR CHIPS

Making homemade chips is a fun way to use up leftover corn or flour tortillas. By adjusting the seasonings, you can create different flavor combinations, from sweet to spicy. The tortilla chips are great for salsa or guacamole (try them with Taco Hummus, page 59) and the cinnamon sugar crisps taste great by themselves, or with Fruit Salsa (page 55).

5 INGREDIENTS OR LESS
30-MINUTE MEAL
NUT-FREE
VEGETARIAN

SERVES 4
PREP TIME: 10 MINUTES
COOK TIME: 15 MINUTES

EQUIPMENT:
Cutting board
Pizza cutter
Small bowl
Spoon
Measuring spoons
Silicone pastry brush
Baking sheet
Oven mitts

INGREDIENTS:
FOR THE TORTILLA CHIPS
5 (6-inch) corn tortillas
2 tablespoons vegetable oil
1 teaspoon freshly
   squeezed lime juice
1 teaspoon chili powder
½ teaspoon salt

 HELPING HAND: Let your helper know you'll need assistance with step 4.

1. Preheat the oven to 350°F.

2. Prep the tortillas.

   Place the tortillas onto a cutting board. Using a pizza cutter, cut each into 8 wedges (like a pizza). Arrange the wedges on a baking sheet in a single layer.

3. To make the tortilla chips: In a small bowl, stir together the oil, lime juice, chili powder, and salt. Using a silicone pastry brush, lightly brush both sides of the tortilla wedges with the oil mixture.

5 (10-inch) flour tortillas
¼ cup sugar
1 tablespoon ground
   cinnamon
2 to 3 tablespoons
   vegetable oil

To make the cinnamon sugar chips:
In a small bowl, stir together the sugar and
cinnamon. Using a silicon pastry brush, lightly
brush the tops of the tortilla wedges with oil.
Sprinkle each with cinnamon sugar.

4. **To bake the tortilla chips:**

Place the baking sheet with the tortilla chips
in the oven and bake for 8 minutes. Using
oven mitts, rotate the pan and bake for 5 to
7 minutes more, or until the chips are crispy
but not too brown.

To bake the cinnamon sugar chips:
Place the baking sheet with the cinnamon
sugar chips in the oven and bake for 4 minutes.
Using oven mitts, rotate the pan and bake
for 4 to 5 minutes more, or until the chips
are crispy but not too brown. The chips will
continue to firm up while they cool.

5. **Serve.**

Serve as-is, or offer salsa or guacamole with the
tortilla chips or fruit salsa with the cinnamon
sugar chips.

Hot Dog Bites,
page 73

OVEN-GRILLED CHEESE SANDWICHES

Why make grilled cheese in a pan when you can bake four at once to crispy, cheesy perfection right in the oven? Change up the flavor by swapping mayo for the butter or using a different type of cheese.

5 INGREDIENTS OR LESS
30-MINUTE MEAL
NUT-FREE
VEGETARIAN

SERVES 4
PREP TIME: 10 MINUTES
COOK TIME: 12 MINUTES

EQUIPMENT:
Butter knife
Baking sheet
Oven mitts
Flipper

INGREDIENTS:
8 slices whole-wheat bread or white bread
4 tablespoons (½ stick) salted butter, divided, at room temperature
4 to 8 slices cheese, such as Cheddar, Swiss, or provolone
Sliced tomato, for filling (optional)
Pickles, for filling (optional)
Sliced deli meat, for filling (optional)

 HELPING HAND: Let your helper know you'll need assistance with step 4.

1. Preheat the oven to 450°F.

2. Prepare the bread.

   Place the bread on a clean work surface. Spread about 1½ teaspoons of butter on one side of each slice of bread (the butter is what makes the bread turn golden brown when cooked).

3. Assemble the sandwiches.

   Arrange 4 slices of bread, buttered-side down, on a baking sheet. Top each with an equal amount of cheese and any fillings you're using. Cover each with the remaining bread slices, buttered-side up.

4. **Bake.**

   Transfer the baking sheet to the preheated oven. Bake for 6 minutes. Using oven mitts, carefully remove the sheet from the oven and then flip the sandwiches over. Return the pan to the oven (still using oven mitts, as the pan is still hot!) and bake for 6 minutes more, or until the cheese melts. Let the sandwiches cool for a few minutes before serving.

SINGLE-SERVE MAC AND CHEESE

Mac and cheese is a popular lunch choice. With this recipe, you can make a single serving easily in your microwave that tastes way better than the boxed kind!

5 INGREDIENTS OR LESS
30-MINUTE MEAL
NUT-FREE
VEGETARIAN

SERVES 1
PREP TIME: 10 MINUTES
COOK TIME: 8 MINUTES

EQUIPMENT:
Measuring cups
  and spoons
Medium
  microwave-safe bowl
Wooden spoon
Oven mitts

INGREDIENTS:
¾ cup water
½ cup dried elbow noodles
⅓ cup shredded sharp
  Cheddar cheese
1 to 2 tablespoons milk
½ teaspoon salted butter
Salt

 HELPING HAND: Let your helper know you'll need assistance with step 1.

1. **Cook the pasta.**

   In a medium microwave-safe bowl, combine the water and elbow noodles. Microwave on high power for 2 minutes. Stir to break apart any clumps of noodles. Return the bowl to the microwave and heat in 2-minute increments, stirring between each, for a total of 6 to 8 minutes, or until the water is fully absorbed. Using oven mitts, carefully remove the bowl from the microwave.

2. **Add the remaining ingredients.**

   Add the Cheddar cheese, milk, and butter to the cooked pasta. Stir well until the cheese melts. Taste and season with salt, if you like.

MIX IT UP: Not in the mood for mac and cheese? Use ¼ cup jarred pasta sauce, pesto sauce, or Alfredo sauce in place of the cheese, milk, and butter.

CHICKEN DIPPERS ON A STICK

These dippers are a fun twist on traditional chicken nuggets. You insert ice pop sticks into the nuggets before cooking, making dipping easier—and more fun! My kids like eating these plain, or with ketchup, but barbecue sauce and ranch dressing pair well, too.

30-MINUTE MEAL
NUT-FREE

MAKES 15 DIPPERS
PREP TIME: 15 MINUTES
COOK TIME: 15 MINUTES

EQUIPMENT:

Baking sheet
Medium bowl
Spoon
Measuring cups
  and spoons
Wooden ice-pop sticks
Flipper
Meat thermometer

INGREDIENTS:

1 pound ground chicken or
  ground turkey
¼ cup shredded
  Cheddar cheese
3 tablespoons
  all-purpose flour
1 teaspoon garlic powder
1 teaspoon onion powder
½ teaspoon chili powder
½ teaspoon salt
Ketchup, barbecue sauce,
  or ranch dressing, for
  dipping (optional)

 HELPING HAND: Let your helper know you'll need assistance with steps 4 and 5.

1. **Preheat the oven to 350°F.**

2. **Combine the ingredients.**

   In a medium bowl, combine the ground chicken, Cheddar cheese, flour, garlic powder, onion powder, chili powder, and salt. Stir well, or mix using your clean hands (wash them right after mixing without touching anything) to combine.

3. **Shape the dippers.**

   Scoop about 2 tablespoons of the chicken mixture into your clean hands and roll it into a ball. Gently shape the ball into a chicken nugget shape and place it on a baking sheet. Repeat to form 15 chicken dippers.

4. **Add the sticks.**

   Gently push 1 ice pop stick into one end of each chicken dipper, about halfway through.

5. **Bake.**

   Transfer the pan to the preheated oven and bake for 10 minutes. Flip the dippers and cook for 5 minutes more. Insert a meat thermometer into the center of a dipper to make sure the internal temperature reaches 165°F (check a couple pieces to ensure proper heating throughout the pan). If the dippers are not hot enough, continue to cook in 2-minute increments until you reach 165°F.

6. **Enjoy.**

   Serve the dippers plain, or with your favorite dipping sauces.

FUN FACT: Did you know kids have more taste buds than adults?

LOADED BAKED POTATOES

Making loaded baked potatoes at home is easy and delicious! If you decide to make these for your family, double the recipe and arrange the toppings in separate bowls so everyone can build their own. Feel free to use this as a jumping-off point: Add cooked crumbled bacon or diced ham, leftover cooked veggies, or any type of cheese you like.

30-MINUTE MEAL
NUT-FREE
VEGETARIAN

SERVES 2
PREP TIME: 10 MINUTES
COOK TIME: 13 MINUTES

EQUIPMENT:
Fork
2 microwave-safe plates
Tongs
Medium
 microwave-safe bowl
Knife
Oven mitts
Colander

INGREDIENTS:
2 russet or Idaho potatoes
½ cup broccoli florets
1 tablespoon water
2 tablespoons salted butter
2 tablespoons sour cream
2 tablespoons shredded
 cheese of choice

 HELPING HAND: Let your helper know you'll need assistance with steps 2, 3, and 4.

1. **Prepare the potatoes.**

   Using the tines of a fork, poke the potatoes several times to create holes (this helps hot air escape while cooking, so the skin doesn't explode).

2. **Cook the potatoes.**

   Place the potatoes on a microwave-safe plate. Microwave on high power for 5 minutes. Using tongs, carefully flip the potatoes over and cook for 5 minutes more, or until the potatoes are soft. Check by poking the potatoes with a fork or paring knife; it should go through the potato with no resistance.

3. Steam the broccoli.

Use your hands to break larger broccoli florets into bite-size pieces. Put the broccoli into a microwave-safe bowl, add the water, and cover the bowl with a small microwave-safe plate. Microwave on high power for 2 to 3 minutes, or until the broccoli is tender (check with a fork or paring knife) but still bright green. Using oven mitts, remove the dish from the microwave. Be careful when removing the plate on top; the steam will be hot. Place a colander in the sink and drain the broccoli in it. Set aside.

4. Open the potato.

Carefully cut open the potato by making a long lengthwise cut, taking care not to get burned by the escaping steam.

5. Add the garnishes.

Top each potato with 1 tablespoon of butter, 1 tablespoon of sour cream, 1 tablespoon of cheese, and half the broccoli.

HOT DOG BITES

Crescent dough turns a plain old hot dog into an exciting handheld lunch that's fun to dip. Crescent dough add a buttery flavor, but you could also use uncooked pizza dough. My daughter enjoys placing two hot dog pieces onto a square then topping it with another square, making ravioli-shaped bites. Be creative!

5 INGREDIENTS OR LESS
30-MINUTE MEAL
NUT-FREE

MAKES 24 BITES
PREP TIME: 15 MINUTES
COOK TIME: 9 MINUTES

EQUIPMENT:
Large cutting board
Baking sheet
Pizza cutter
Knife
Small spoon

INGREDIENTS:
2 turkey hot dogs
1 (8-ounce) tube
  refrigerated
  crescent dough
Ketchup, for dipping
Mustard, for dipping

 HELPING HAND: Let your helper know you'll need assistance with step 5.

1. Preheat the oven to 375°F.

2. Prepare the hot dogs.

   Cut each hot dog into 12 even coin-shaped pieces.

3. Prepare the crescent dough.

   Using the back of a spoon, pop open the can of dough (follow the directions on the package). Unroll the crescent dough and place it on a large cutting board or clean work surface with the long (horizontal) side facing you. Using a pizza cutter, cut the dough into quarters horizontally, and into sixths vertically, creating 24 squares.

continued >>

4. **Assemble the bites.**

   Place 1 hot dog coin on each of the 24 squares. Wrap the dough around the hot dog, folding two opposite corners in, then the other corners. Using your hands, gently pinch closed all the gaps in the dough. Transfer the wrapped coins to a baking sheet.

5. **Bake.**

   Transfer the baking sheet to the preheated oven and bake for 9 minutes, or until the dough is golden brown. Serve plain, or with ketchup and mustard for dipping.

NO-BAKE TOSTADAS

Tostadas are a fun, handheld lunch that's sort of like eating a flat, crunchy taco! You can add any vegetables you like, or try swapping the beans for shredded chicken or beef.

30-MINUTE MEAL
NUT-FREE
VEGETARIAN

SERVES 2
PREP TIME: 20 MINUTES
COOK TIME: 1 MINUTE

EQUIPMENT:
Can opener
Cutting board
Knife
Spoon
Measuring cups
  and spoons
Microwave-safe plate
Oven mitts

INGREDIENTS:
2 (6-inch) tostadas
¼ cup canned vegetarian
  refried beans
2 tablespoons finely
  shredded Mexican-style
  blend cheese or
  Cheddar cheese
½ cup shredded lettuce
1 tomato, diced
¼ cup salsa

 HELPING HAND: Let your helper know you'll need assistance with step 2.

1. **Prep the tostadas.**

   Place the tostadas on a clean work surface. Carefully spread 2 tablespoons of refried beans over each. Sprinkle 1 tablespoon of shredded cheese on top of each.

2. **Microwave.**

   Transfer the tostadas to a microwave-safe plate. Cook on high power for 45 seconds. Using oven mitts, remove the plate from the microwave.

3. **Top the tostadas.**

   Top the warm tostadas with lettuce, tomato, and salsa to serve.

MIX IT UP: Don't like refried beans? Try leftover taco meat, or shredded chicken or beef, instead.

STACK IT UP SANDWICH

This stacked-up sandwich takes peanut butter to a new level of yum! And it's so big that it's perfect for sharing with a sibling or friend. It's easy to make more if you're serving a crowd; just multiply the recipe.

10 MINUTES OR LESS
NO HELP NEEDED
VEGETARIAN

SERVES 2
PREP TIME: 10 MINUTES

EQUIPMENT:
Cutting board
Knife
Measuring spoons
Butter knife
Plate

INGREDIENTS:
1 small banana
2 or 3 fresh strawberries
2 tablespoons smooth
  peanut butter
3 slices cinnamon-
  raisin bread
1 tablespoon sweetened
  shredded coconut
Honey, for drizzling

1. **Prepare the fruit.**

   Peel the banana and place it on a cutting board. Cut the banana into even, bite-size slices. Set aside. Cut the top off each strawberry and cut each berry into 3 even slices.

2. **Make the first layer.**

   Spread the peanut butter onto 1 slice of bread. Evenly arrange the banana slices over the peanut butter.

3. **Make the second layer.**

   Cover the bananas with another slice of bread. Arrange the strawberry slices on top, then sprinkle with the coconut and drizzle with honey.

4. **Finish the sandwich.**

   Cover the sandwich with the remaining slice of bread. Cut the sandwich diagonally, then diagonally again, creating 4 triangles, and serve.

   FUN FACT: Peanuts (specifically, peanut oil) are an ingredient in dynamite!

CAESAR SALAD WITH HOMEMADE PARMESAN CROUTONS

If there's one salad my kids can agree on, it's Caesar salad, a creamy, garlicky, delicious combo of crisp lettuce and crunchy homemade croutons. Croutons are very easy to make and are a great use for leftover bread. They add a wonderful crunch to this salad. If you don't have time to make homemade croutons, substitute store-bought croutons.

30-MINUTE MEAL
NUT-FREE

SERVES 4
PREP TIME: 15 MINUTES
COOK TIME: 14 MINUTES

EQUIPMENT:
Cutting board
Knife
Baking sheet
Oven mitts
Flipper
Vegetable peeler
Measuring spoons
Bowls: medium and small
Spoon
Salad servers
Serving bowl

INGREDIENTS:
FOR THE CROUTONS
4 slices French bread, whole-wheat bread, or white bread (1- to 2-day-old bread works best)

 HELPING HAND: Let your helper know you'll need assistance with steps 2 through 4.

1. Preheat the oven to 375°F.
2. To make the croutons: On a cutting board, cut the bread into ½- to 1-inch cubes. Spread them on a baking sheet.
3. Bake the croutons.

Transfer the baking sheet to the preheated oven and bake the bread cubes for 7 minutes. Using oven mitts, remove the baking sheet from the oven, flip the cubes over, and bake for 7 minutes more until crisp.

continued >>

3 tablespoons olive oil

1 tablespoon grated
  Parmesan cheese

½ teaspoon garlic powder

½ teaspoon onion powder

Pinch salt

Dash freshly ground
  black pepper

FOR THE SALAD
INGREDIENTS

1 large head Romaine
  lettuce, torn into
  bite-size pieces

¼ cup freshly shaved
  Parmesan cheese (use a
  vegetable peeler to shave
  the cheese from a block)

1 teaspoon freshly ground
  black pepper (optional)

¼ cup bottled Caesar salad
  dressing

4. **Prepare the crouton seasoning.**

   In a small bowl, stir together the oil, Parmesan cheese, garlic powder, onion powder, salt, and pepper to combine. Pour this mixture over the bread cubes on the baking sheet, stirring well to coat all the croutons.

5. **To make the salad:** In a large salad bowl, combine the romaine lettuce, Parmesan cheese, pepper, Caesar dressing, and croutons. Gently toss with salad servers or two mixing spoons and serve.

MIX IT UP: Make the salad more filling by adding sliced hard-boiled eggs or shredded cooked chicken.

NAAN PIZZA TWO WAYS

This pizza recipe features naan flatbread topped two ways so you can have your pizza just the way you like it! If you're making this for your family for dinner, ask each family member which kind of toppings they'd like—it's easy to please everyone!

30-MINUTE MEAL	SERVES 2
NUT-FREE	PREP TIME: 20 MINUTES
VEGETARIAN	COOK TIME: 8 MINUTES

EQUIPMENT:
Silicone pastry brush
Cutting board
Knife
Measuring cups and spoons
Baking sheet
Oven mitts

INGREDIENTS:
FOR THE MEDITERRANEAN PIZZA
2 (6-inch) whole-wheat naan breads
1 tablespoon olive oil
1 teaspoon bottled minced garlic
½ cup shredded mozzarella cheese
¼ cup shredded Parmesan cheese
¼ cup oil-packed sliced sundried tomatoes, drained
¼ cup arugula
⅛ teaspoon red pepper flakes

 HELPING HAND: Let your helper know you'll need assistance with step 3.

1. Preheat the oven to 350°F.

2. Prepare the pizzas.

   To make the Mediterranean naan pizza: Brush the naan with oil. Sprinkle with the garlic and top with the mozzarella and Parmesan cheeses. Evenly arrange the sundried tomato slices over the cheese, top with the arugula, and sprinkle with red pepper flakes.

   To make the veggie naan pizza: Evenly spread the pizza sauce over the naan. Sprinkle with the mozzarella cheese and arrange the green bell pepper and mushrooms on top. Scatter the tomato over the toppings.

continued >>

FOR THE VEGGIE PIZZA

½ cup pizza sauce or
   marinara sauce
2 (6-inch) whole-wheat
   naan breads
½ cup shredded
   mozzarella cheese
½ green bell pepper, sliced
¼ cup sliced mushrooms
1 tomato, diced (optional)

3. Bake.

Carefully place the naan pizzas on a baking
sheet and transfer the baking sheet to the
preheated oven. Bake for 8 minutes, or until
the cheese melts.

CHICKEN TAQUITOS

This handheld lunch is made with corn tortillas baked into delicious, crispy rolls. They're just as fun to eat as they are delicious.

5 INGREDIENTS OR LESS
30-MINUTE MEAL
NUT-FREE

SERVES 2
PREP TIME: 15 MINUTES
COOKING TIME: 13 MINUTES

EQUIPMENT:
Wire rack that fits on a
  baking sheet
Baking sheet
Measuring cups
  and spoons
Medium bowl
Spoon
4 pieces paper towel
Microwave-safe plate

INGREDIENTS:
⅔ cup shredded
  cooked chicken
¼ cup shredded
  Mexican-style blend
  cheese or sharp
  Cheddar cheese
¼ cup salsa
4 (4½-inch) corn tortillas
Nonstick cooking spray

 HELPING HAND: Let your helper know you'll need assistance with steps 4 and 6.

1. **Preheat the oven to 400° F.**

   Place a wire rack on top of a baking sheet.

2. **Combine the ingredients.**

   In a medium bowl, stir together the chicken, cheese, and salsa to combine. Set aside.

3. **Prepare the tortillas.**

   Fold 4 pieces of paper towel on top of each other and run the stack under water. Gently squeeze the wet towels to remove excess water. Open the damp paper towels and place the corn tortillas between the sheets. Wrap the towels around the tortillas and place them on a microwave-safe plate.

4. **Heat the tortillas.**

   Microwave the corn tortillas on high power for 25 seconds. Have your helper remove the tortillas from the microwave, as they will be hot. Unwrap and remove one tortilla, keeping the others covered. Place the tortilla on a clean work surface.

5. **Assemble the taquitos.**

Place one-fourth of the chicken mixture into the middle of the tortilla. Wrap the bottom of the tortilla around the mixture, gently pulling it toward you, then roll it up the rest of the way. Place the taquito, seam-side down, onto the wire rack. Spray the taquito with cooking spray. Repeat with the remaining 3 tortillas and filling.

6. **Bake.**

Transfer the baking sheet with the rack to the preheated oven and bake for 10 to 12 minutes, until the taquitos are crispy and lightly browned.

MIX IT UP: Corn tortillas can be a little fragile (they tend to break when they're cold), but microwaving them in a damp paper towel prevents them from breaking. If the tortillas do break, remove the chicken mixture and start with new tortillas. Don't have corn tortillas? Use flour tortillas.

SOUTHWESTERN QUESADILLAS

Flour tortillas can be transformed into crispy, cheesy quesadillas in just a few simple steps. Quesadillas have been a staple at my house since my children were toddlers. Sometimes we make them plain with cheese; sometimes we add refried beans and chicken. Try both versions to see which is your favorite.

30-MINUTE MEAL
NUT-FREE

SERVES 4
PREP TIME: 10 MINUTES
COOK TIME: 6 MINUTES
PER QUESADILLA

EQUIPMENT:

Can opener
Spoon
Measuring cups
  and spoons
Electric griddle or skillet
Flipper
Pizza cutter

INGREDIENTS:

8 (8-inch) whole-wheat
  tortillas
½ cup canned vegetarian
  refried beans
¾ cup shredded
  cooked chicken
1 cup shredded
  Cheddar cheese
4 teaspoons vegetable
  oil, divided
Salsa, for serving (optional)
Sour cream, for serving
  (optional)

 HELPING HAND: Have your helper assist with steps 3 and 4.

1. **Prepare the quesadillas.**

   Place 4 tortillas on a clean work surface. Evenly spread about 2 tablespoons of refried beans onto each tortilla. Top each with about 2 tablespoons of chicken and ¼ cup of Cheddar cheese. Place another tortilla on top of the fillings.

2. **Preheat.**

   Heat a griddle to 350°F, or place a medium skillet over medium-high heat. Add 1 teaspoon of oil to the griddle or skillet and let it heat for about 1 minute.

3. Cook.

Carefully place one quesadilla onto the griddle. Cook for 2 to 3 minutes until the bottom is browned (peek using a spatula). Carefully flip the tortilla over and cook for 2 to 3 minutes more, or until it's golden brown and the cheese is melted. Transfer it to a cutting board. Repeat this process with the remaining 3 quesadillas.

4. Slice.

Using a pizza cutter, cut each quesadilla into 6 wedges. Serve topped with salsa (if using) and sour cream (if using).

MIX IT UP: Don't have shredded chicken? Substitute 1 (4½-ounce) can white chunk chicken, drained. If you don't want to use the stovetop, place a quesadilla onto a microwave-safe plate and microwave it, one quesadilla at a time, on high power for about 1 minute until the cheese melts.

TURKEY "SUSHI"

Turkey "sushi" takes the turkey sandwich to a whole new level. Deli turkey is wrapped around cheese, spinach, and carrot and spread with your favorite sauce to make bite-size pieces that are fun to eat with chopsticks.

10 MINUTES OR LESS
NO HELP NEEDED
NUT-FREE

SERVES 1
PREP TIME: 10 MINUTES

EQUIPMENT:
Measuring spoons
Butter knife
Knife
Chopsticks

INGREDIENTS:
1 large (10-inch)
   whole-grain flour tortilla
1 to 2 tablespoons of your
   favorite sauce (hummus,
   ranch, mayonnaise, etc.)
½ cup shredded
   mozzarella cheese
4 or 5 fresh spinach leaves
3 or 4 thin slices deli turkey
½ cup shredded carrot

1. **Prepare the tortilla.**

   Place the tortilla on a clean work surface. Spread it evenly with your preferred sauce.

2. **Add the toppings.**

   Sprinkle the mozzarella cheese over the sauce. Top with the spinach, then turkey. Place the carrots in a horizontal line across the tortilla.

3. **Roll the tortilla.**

   Starting at the end of the tortilla with the carrot, carefully roll the tortilla over itself, rolling tightly as you go.

4. **Cut the "sushi."**

   Cut your roll into 5 or 6 even pieces. Eat with chopsticks, if desired.

MIX IT UP: Use ham, roast beef, or just veggies to create a whole new kind of "sushi." You can find shredded carrot at the grocery store or shred your own using a box grater.

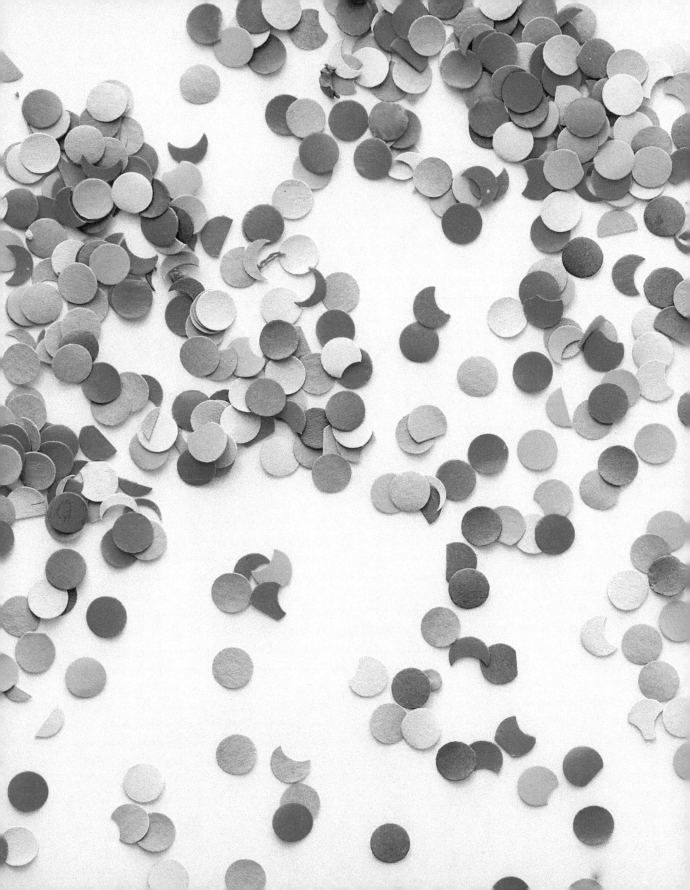

Baked Ravioli,
page 104

CHEESEBURGER SLIDERS

A "slider" is a mini sandwich. These cheeseburger sliders come together quickly and are baked for the perfect combination of toasty bread, tasty meatballs, and cheesy deliciousness!

5 INGREDIENTS OR LESS
30-MINUTE MEAL
NUT-FREE

MAKES 12 MEATBALL SLIDERS
PREP TIME: 15 MINUTES
COOK TIME: 7 MINUTES

EQUIPMENT:

Medium microwave-
   safe bowl
Meat thermometer
Serrated knife
9-by-13-inch baking pan
Measuring spoons
Flipper

INGREDIENTS:

12 frozen meatballs
12 sweet dinner rolls
   (I like King's Hawaiian)
6 slices Cheddar cheese,
   cut in half
12 pickle slices
Ketchup, for topping

 HELPING HAND: Let your helper know you'll need assistance with steps 3 and 5.

1. Preheat the oven to 350°F.
2. Cook the meatballs.

   Place the meatballs into a medium microwave-safe bowl. Microwave on high power for 2 minutes, or until the meatballs are heated through (you can check by carefully touching them to see if they are hot, or use a meat thermometer and heat until the meatballs reach an internal temperature of 140°F).

3. Prepare the rolls.

   Using a serrated knife, carefully cut the dinner rolls in half, separating top from bottom. Arrange the bun bottoms, cut-side up, in a single layer in a 9-by-13 baking pan.

4. **Top the buns.**

Place 1 meatball on each bun bottom. Top with ½ slice of cheese, folded in half (to form a square), 1 pickle slice, and about 1 teaspoon of ketchup per slider. Cover with the bun tops.

5. **Bake.**

Transfer the baking pan to the preheated oven and bake for 5 to 7 minutes, or just until the cheese melts.

MIX IT UP: Make these sliders into "Big Mac-style" sliders by adding 1 teaspoon Thousand Island dressing to the top of each slider before baking. Once they're out of the oven, sprinkle each slider with a little shredded lettuce.

EASY CHICKEN TORTILLA SOUP

This chicken tortilla soup comes together quickly with the use of pantry staples. If you'd like extra black beans or corn, simply use two cans instead of one. (At my house we like one can of black beans and two cans of corn.) My kids love topping tortilla soup with lots of cheese and tortilla chips; my favorite way is with a little plain Greek yogurt and chopped scallion on top.

NUT-FREE

SERVES AT LEAST 4
PREP TIME: 15 MINUTES
COOK TIME: 25 MINUTES

EQUIPMENT:
Can opener
Stockpot
Measuring cups
  and spoons
Wooden spoon
Ladle

INGREDIENTS:
8 cups low-sodium
  chicken broth
2 to 3 cups shredded
  cooked chicken, or
  2 (10-ounce) cans
  chicken, drained
1 or 2 (15-ounce) cans black
  beans, rinsed and drained
1 or 2 (15-ounce) cans
  corn, rinsed and drained,
  or 1 to 2 cups frozen
  corn kernels
1 (10-ounce) can diced
  tomatoes and green
  chilies (I like Ro-Tel)

 HELPING HAND: Let your helper know you'll need assistance with opening the cans and step 1.

1. **Combine the ingredients.**

   In a stockpot over medium heat, stir together the chicken broth, chicken, black beans, corn, tomatoes and green chilies, and enchilada sauce.

2. **Simmer the soup.**

   Bring the soup to a boil. Reduce the heat to low and simmer the soup for about 15 minutes.

3. **Garnish the soup.**

   Serve the soup topped with crushed tortilla chips and any additional toppings, as desired.

continued >>

1 (10-ounce) can mild red enchilada sauce

½ to 1 cup tortilla chips, crushed

Cilantro, for topping (optional)

Sour cream or plain Greek yogurt, for topping (optional)

Shredded cheese of choice, for topping (optional)

Sliced scallions, for topping (optional)

MIX IT UP: Make this soup vegetarian. Omit the chicken, use vegetable broth instead of chicken broth, and add an extra can of beans, corn, and tomatoes.

DAD'S DELICIOUS ONE-POT SPAGHETTI

Spaghetti is the one meal my husband makes that wins against mine. His secret? Cut the meatballs in half before adding them to the pot so you get a meatball with every bite! If you want to do this, thaw the meatballs before you cut them—otherwise, it's okay to add them to the pot whole.

30-MINUTE MEAL
NUT-FREE

SERVES 6
PREP TIME: 10 MINUTES
COOK TIME: 20 MINUTES

EQUIPMENT:
Stockpot
Measuring cups
Wooden spoon
Knife
Tongs

INGREDIENTS:
1 (32-ounce) jar
    spaghetti sauce
1 (28-ounce) can crushed
    tomatoes
1 cup water
1 (16-ounce) package
    dried spaghetti noodles,
    broken in half
1 (24-ounce) bag frozen
    Italian-style meatballs
1 cup shredded
    mozzarella cheese
5 to 10 fresh basil leaves, or
    1 teaspoon dried basil

 HELPING HAND: Let your helper know you'll need assistance throughout.

1. **Combine the ingredients.**

   In a stockpot over high heat, stir together the spaghetti sauce, tomatoes, water, spaghetti, and meatballs. Bring to a boil.

2. **Simmer the pasta.**

   Reduce the heat to medium-low, cover the pot with a lid, and cook for 15 to 20 minutes, stirring often, or until the spaghetti is just tender (this is called al dente).

3. **Finish the pasta.**

   Turn off the heat under the stockpot. Stir in the cheese and basil. Stir well and serve.

ONE-MINUTE MICROWAVE PIZZA

At my house, these pizzas are a summertime staple because you don't need an oven to cook them—a microwave works great!

5 INGREDIENTS OR LESS
30-MINUTE MEAL
NUT-FREE

SERVES 4
PREP TIME: 15 MINUTES
COOK TIME: 4 MINUTES

EQUIPMENT:

Spoon
Cutting board
4 (8-ounce)
  ramekins or small
  microwave-safe bowls
Measuring cups
Knife
Oven mitts

INGREDIENTS:

1 (13.8-ounce) tube
  refrigerated pizza dough
¼ cup pizza sauce
¾ cup shredded
  mozzarella cheese
½ green bell
  pepper, chopped
¼ cup mini
  pepperoni slices

 HELPING HAND: Let your helper know you'll need assistance with step 3.

1. **Prepare the dough.**

   Using the back of a spoon, pop open the can of dough (follow the directions on the package). Unroll the pizza dough on a cutting board. Flip an 8-ounce ramekin or a small, microwave-safe bowl upside-down and use it as a cookie cutter to cut out a crust. Once cut, flip the ramekin or bowl right-side up and gently place the cut pizza dough into the bottom of it. Repeat for the remaining 3 pizzas.

2. **Assemble the pizzas.**

   Using a spoon, evenly divide the pizza sauce among the 4 crusts, spreading it evenly over the dough. Sprinkle each with an equal amount of cheese, then top with green bell pepper and pepperoni slices.

3. **Microwave the pizzas.**

Place 1 pizza into the microwave. Cook on high power for 1 minute. Using oven mitts, carefully remove the pizza from the microwave. Repeat with the remaining pizzas. Let the pizzas cool slightly before serving.

MIX IT UP: Switch up the toppings on your pizza to customize it to your liking. Try cooked sausage, chopped tomato, sliced mushrooms, or different cheeses.

FUN FACT: Over five billion pizzas are sold worldwide each year!

HOMEMADE CHICKEN NOODLE SOUP

Homemade chicken soup is a favorite at my house. With this simplified version, you get a flavorful veggie-packed soup. If you're in a hurry, steam the carrots in the microwave until soft before adding them to the soup to cut the cook time.

NUT-FREE

SERVES 4 TO 6
PREP TIME: 20 MINUTES
COOK TIME: 45 MINUTES

EQUIPMENT:
Stockpot
Cutting board
Knife
Measuring cups and spoons
Wooden spoon

INGREDIENTS:
1 tablespoon olive oil
1 large onion, diced
1 (1-pound) bag
   sliced carrots
4 or 5 celery stalks, sliced
2 teaspoons poultry
   seasoning
2 teaspoons garlic powder
1 to 2 teaspoons salt
1 bay leaf (fresh or dried)
8 cups reduced-sodium
   chicken broth
2 cups shredded
   cooked chicken
1 cup dried egg noodles

 HELPING HAND: This recipe needs a helper for all steps. Your helper can assist you with chopping the veggies, bringing the soup to a boil, and serving once it's finished cooking. There is a 30-minute break while the soup simmers.

1. **Cook the onion.**

   In a stockpot over medium-high heat, heat the oil until it shimmers. Add the onion. Cook for 4 to 5 minutes, stirring occasionally, until the onion looks translucent.

2. **Add the vegetables.**

   Stir in the carrots, celery, poultry seasoning, garlic powder, 1 teaspoon of salt, the bay leaf, and chicken broth. Turn the heat to high and bring the soup to a boil.

3. **Simmer the soup.**

   Reduce the heat to medium and simmer the soup for 30 minutes.

4. **Finish the soup.**

   Stir in the chicken and egg noodles. Simmer the soup for 10 to 15 minutes more, or until the carrots are soft and the noodles are cooked. Taste and add more salt, if needed.

   FUN FACT: Studies show that chicken soup can help strengthen the body's immune response to help you fight off cold viruses.

ALEX'S FAMOUS BURRITOS

When my son, Alex, was about eight years old, he wanted to invent his own dinner. Five years later, we can still make his recipe because he wrote it down. When you start getting comfortable in the kitchen, feel free to make ingredient swaps or change the quantities of the ingredients to make your own recipes. Write each one down so you can make your recipes again and again!

NUT-FREE

SERVES 4
PREP TIME: 20 MINUTES
COOK TIME: 15 MINUTES

EQUIPMENT:
Cutting board
Knife
Measuring cups
 and spoons
Large skillet
Wooden spoon
Spatula
Small bowl

INGREDIENTS:
1 tablespoon olive oil
1 small onion, diced
½ green bell pepper, diced
1 pound bulk pork sausage
1 teaspoon onion powder
½ teaspoon salt
¼ teaspoon black pepper
⅛ teaspoon red
 pepper flakes
1 tomato, diced
4 (10-inch) whole-wheat
 tortillas
⅔ cup shredded sharp
 Cheddar cheese

 HELPING HAND: Let your helper know you'll need assistance with steps 1 and 2.

1. **Sauté the vegetables.**

   In a large skillet over medium-high heat, heat the oil until it shimmers. Add the onion and green bell pepper. Cook for 4 minutes, stirring occasionally, or until the onion starts to soften.

2. **Cook the meat.**

   Add the sausage and break up the meat with your spoon. Cook over medium-high heat for about 5 minutes, stirring occasionally, until no pink remains. Turn off the heat and ask your helper to assist you in carefully draining the liquid from the pan into a bowl. To do this, lift and tilt the skillet above a small bowl while holding a spatula or spoon at the bottom, pressing against the meat and vegetables to keep them from falling out, or use a colander.

3. **Season the meat.**

   Return the skillet with the meat mixture to the heat and add the onion powder, salt, black pepper, and red pepper flakes. Stir in the diced tomato. Cook for 1 minute more, then remove the skillet from the heat.

4. **Assemble the burritos.**

   Place the tortillas on a clean work surface. Evenly divide the meat mixture among the tortillas. Top each with Cheddar cheese. Fold in the sides, then fold the bottom over and roll up the tortillas into a burrito.

5. **Heat the burritos.**

   If desired, place each burrito on a microwave-safe plate and heat, one at a time, in the microwave on high power for 40 to 60 seconds until the cheese melts.

MIX IT UP: Swap ground beef or ground turkey for the pork or use Mexican-style cheese in place of the Cheddar. Top the burritos with salsa, black olives, sliced scallion, or sour cream if you like.

BAKED RAVIOLI

In this recipe, frozen ravioli are dipped into an egg wash, coated in bread crumbs and Parmesan cheese, then baked to perfection! This twist creates ravioli that are crispy on the outside and cheesy on the inside. Eat them plain or dipped in pizza sauce for a fun dinner.

30-MINUTE MEAL
NUT-FREE
VEGETARIAN

MAKES 24 RAVIOLI
PREP TIME: 15 MINUTES
COOK TIME: 12 MINUTES

EQUIPMENT:
Wire rack
Rimmed sheet pan
2 shallow, wide-bottom
  bowls or pans
Measuring cups
  and spoons
Spoon
Fork
Tongs

INGREDIENTS:
Nonstick cooking spray
1 cup panko bread crumbs
¼ cup shredded
  Parmesan cheese
½ teaspoon dried basil
½ teaspoon dried oregano
2 large eggs
24 frozen cheese ravioli
  (do not thaw)
1 cup pizza sauce or
  marinara sauce

 HELPING HAND: Let your helper know you'll need assistance with step 6.

1. **Preheat the oven to 375°F.**

   Place a wire rack on a rimmed baking sheet. Coat the wire rack with cooking spray. Set aside.

2. **Prepare the breading.**

   In a shallow, wide-bottom bowl or pan, stir together the panko, Parmesan cheese, basil, and oregano.

3. **Prepare the eggs.**

   In another shallow, wide-bottom bowl or pan, crack the eggs, then whisk them with a fork to blend.

4. **Bread the ravioli.**

   Working with one or two ravioli at a time, using tongs, add the frozen ravioli to the whisked eggs, turning to coat both sides in the egg. Using tongs, transfer the ravioli from the eggs to the panko mixture. Use one clean hand to coat the ravioli on both sides with the panko mixture, then place the coated ravioli on the prepared wire rack. Repeat until all the ravioli are coated. Coat the tops of the ravioli with cooking spray.

5. **Bake.**

   Transfer the baking sheet with the wire rack to the preheated oven and bake for 10 to 12 minutes, or until the ravioli are golden brown.

6. **Serve.**

   If you like, warm the sauce in the microwave while the ravioli cook. Serve the ravioli with the sauce for dipping.

SUPER SIMPLE CALZONES

Calzones are like a baked pizza pocket and relatively simple to make. Don't stress if your calzone oozes open while cooking. It's bound to happen to at least a couple of them. It doesn't affect the flavor and I've never gotten a complaint.

30-MINUTE MEAL
NUT-FREE

MAKES 4 CALZONES
PREP TIME: 15 MINUTES
COOK TIME: 13 MINUTES

EQUIPMENT:

Bowls: medium, small
Measuring cups
    and spoons
Spoon
Fork
Cutting board
Pizza cutter
Rolling pin
Silicone pastry brush
Baking sheet

INGREDIENTS:

1 cup frozen turkey sausage
    crumbles
1 cup mini pepperoni slices
1 cup pizza sauce
1 cup shredded
    mozzarella cheese
1 teaspoon Italian
    seasoning, plus more for
    sprinkling
1 large egg
1 (13.8-ounce) tube
    refrigerated pizza dough

 HELPING HAND: Let your helper know you'll need assistance with step 8.

1. **Preheat the oven to 425°F.**
2. **Prepare the filling.**

   In a medium bowl, combine the turkey sausage, pepperoni, pizza sauce, mozzarella cheese, and Italian seasoning. Stir well and set aside.

3. **Make the egg wash.**

   In a small bowl, crack the egg and whisk it with a fork to blend. Set aside.

4. **Prepare the pizza dough.**

   Using the back of a spoon, pop open the can of dough (follow the directions on the package). Unroll the pizza dough onto a cutting board. Using a pizza cutter, cut the dough into 4 equal sections by cutting through the middle horizontally, then vertically.

MIX IT UP: Want to skip the meat? Use mushrooms, bell pepper, and tomato in place of the sausage and pepperoni, or add them all for a supreme calzone.

5. **Roll the dough.**

   Place 3 pieces of dough on a baking sheet, spacing them a few inches apart (leave one on the cutting board). Using a rolling pin, roll the dough on your cutting board until it's about ¼ inch thick but not so thin that you can't fold it over without tearing it.

6. **Assemble the calzones.**

   Place one-fourth of the meat mixture diagonally on the rolled-out pizza crust. Fold the dough over the meat mixture, arranging the bottom crust over the top crust, pressing to seal (use your fingers to make sure the dough is well sealed). Carefully transfer the calzone to the baking sheet. Take another piece of dough and repeat the rolling and assembling until all 4 calzones are assembled.

7. **Finish the calzones.**

   Using a pastry brush or a spoon, spread a little of the beaten egg on top of each calzone. Sprinkle each with Italian seasoning.

8. **Bake.**

   Transfer the baking sheet to the preheated oven and bake for 10 to 13 minutes, or until the tops of the calzones are golden brown.

TERIYAKI RICE BUDDHA BOWL

A Buddha bowl is a one-dish meal consisting of rice, vegetables, dressing, and some type of protein. This version is made simple with packaged rice, vegetables, and canned fish. Switch it up by setting the makings for this Buddha-bowl dinner on the table for your family to assemble as they wish.

30-MINUTE MEAL
NUT-FREE

SERVES 4
PREP TIME: 15 MINUTES
COOK TIME: 12 MINUTES

EQUIPMENT:
Oven mitts
Medium microwave-safe
  bowl (with handle and
  spout if possible)
Measuring cups
  and spoons
Small bowl
Fork
4 individual serving bowls

INGREDIENTS:
2 pouches (4 servings)
  packaged cooked brown
  rice (such as Uncle Ben's
  Ready Rice)
1 (16-ounce) bag
  microwavable frozen
  stir-fry vegetables
1¼ cups cold water, divided
¼ cup reduced-sodium
  soy sauce

 HELPING HAND: Let your helper know you'll need assistance with steps 1 through 5.

1. **Prepare the rice.**

   Microwave the rice according to the package instructions. Using oven mitts, remove the rice from the microwave and set it aside.

2. **Prepare the vegetables.**

   Microwave the vegetables according to the package instructions. Using oven mitts, remove the package from the microwave.

3. **Prepare the sauce.**

   In a medium microwave-safe bowl, with a handle and pour spout if available, stir together 1 cup of cold water, the soy sauce, brown sugar, ginger, and garlic powder. Microwave the soy sauce mixture on high power for 1 minute. Using oven mitts, carefully remove the bowl from the microwave and set it aside.

1½ tablespoons light
   brown sugar
1 teaspoon ground ginger
½ teaspoon garlic powder
2 tablespoons cornstarch
1 (5-ounce) can tuna,
   drained, or 2 (3-ounce)
   pouches salmon
2 scallions, root ends
   trimmed, chopped

4. **Add the cornstarch.**

In a small bowl, combine the cornstarch
and remaining ¼ cup of cold water, stirring
with a fork until well blended. Using the
fork, whisk the cornstarch mixture (called a
slurry) into the heated soy sauce mixture.

5. **Thicken the sauce.**

Put the soy sauce mixture into the
microwave and heat on high power in
1-minute increments, stirring every minute,
for 3 minutes (the sauce should start to
thicken from the slurry as you heat it).

6. **Assemble the bowls.**

Divide the cooked rice, cooked vegetables,
and tuna among 4 bowls. Evenly pour the
sauce over the ingredients in the bowls.

7. **Garnish the bowls.**

Top with the chopped scallions and
serve hot.

MIX IT UP: Don't like fish? Swap the canned
fish for canned chicken or use leftover
chicken, beef, or pork. Max out the veggies
by adding fresh chopped vegetables you
have on hand, such as cucumbers, rad-
ishes, or zucchini.

VEGGIES AND RICE NOODLES WITH PEANUT SAUCE

If you're looking for a delicious, meat-free meal, you're in the right place. This peanut sauce started out as a dressing for green beans, and it is so good, it convinced a number of kids they actually like green beans! It's super versatile and it's the perfect complement for this yummy noodle dish.

30-MINUTE MEAL
VEGETARIAN

SERVES 4
PREP TIME: 10 MINUTES
COOK TIME: 20 MINUTES

EQUIPMENT:

Stockpot
Colander
Oven mitts
Large microwave-safe bowl
    with lid
Measuring cups
    and spoons
Large slotted spoon
Large bowl
Juicer
Whisk
Tongs

INGREDIENTS:

1 (8-ounce) package pad
    thai brown rice noodles
1 (16-ounce) bag frozen
    stir-fry vegetables
5 tablespoons hot
    water, divided
¼ cup smooth
    peanut butter

 HELPING HAND: Let your helper know you'll need assistance with steps 1 and 2.

1. **Cook the noodles.**

   Fill a stockpot with hot water and carefully place it over high heat. Bring to a boil. Add the rice noodles and cook according to the package instructions (this should take about 5 minutes). Place a colander in the sink and drain the noodles (but don't run them under cold water).

2. **Steam the vegetables.**

   Pour the frozen vegetables into a large microwave-safe bowl with a lid (or use a microwave-safe plate to cover the bowl). Add 3 tablespoons of hot water to the vegetables. Cover the bowl and microwave for 8 minutes.

   continued >>

2 tablespoons
 reduced-sodium soy sauce
1 tablespoon freshly
 squeezed lemon juice
1 teaspoon sriracha

Using a large slotted spoon, transfer the vegetables to another bowl, leaving any cooking water behind.

3. **Make the sauce.**

Meanwhile, in a large bowl, whisk the peanut butter, remaining 2 tablespoons of hot water, soy sauce, lemon juice, and sriracha until smooth; it will take a bit of stirring to get the peanut butter to blend in.

4. **Assemble the bowls.**

Using tongs, add the noodles and vegetables to the peanut butter sauce. Toss together to coat and combine. Serve hot.

LOADED NACHO BITES

My daughter could live on nachos. We've tried many varieties over the years. This recipe is my favorite because it results in the perfect bite every time. Individual tortilla chips are spread with a combination of a flavor-packed refried bean mixture, loaded with cheese, and baked to crispy perfection.

30-MINUTE MEAL	SERVES 4	
NUT-FREE	PREP TIME: 15 MINUTES	
VEGETARIAN	COOK TIME: 7 MINUTES	

EQUIPMENT:
Can opener
Medium bowl
Measuring cups
  and spoons
Wooden spoon
Tablespoon
14-by-20-inch baking
  sheet (or 2 smaller
  baking sheets)
Oven mitts

INGREDIENTS:
1 (16-ounce) can vegetarian
  refried beans
½ cup Mexican-style
  canned diced tomatoes (I
  like Ro-Tel), drained
½ teaspoon ground cumin
½ teaspoon chili powder
28 restaurant-style
  tortilla chips
1 cup shredded sharp
  Cheddar or Mexican-style
  blend cheese

 HELPING HAND: Let your helper know you'll need assistance opening the cans and with step 5.

1. Preheat the oven to 350°F.
2. **Make the bean mixture.**

   In a medium bowl, stir together the refried beans, tomatoes, cumin, and chili powder.

3. **Assemble the nachos.**

   Using a 1-tablespoon measuring spoon, scoop and spread 1 tablespoon of the refried bean mixture onto a tortilla chip. Transfer the chip to a baking sheet. Repeat with the remaining tortillas and bean mixture.

4. **Top with cheese.**

   Sprinkle each chip with shredded cheese.

continued >>

1 (12-ounce) container pico de gallo (typically found in the refrigerated section of your grocery store near the produce)

Guacamole, for topping (optional)

Sour cream, for topping (optional)

Sliced black olives, for topping (optional)

Chopped scallion, for topping (optional)

Sliced jalapeño peppers, for topping (optional)

5. **Bake.**

Transfer the baking sheet to the preheated oven and bake the nachos for 5 to 7 minutes, or until the cheese is melted.

6. **Garnish.**

Top the baked nachos with pico de gallo and any additional toppings, as desired.

MIX IT UP: Skip the beans, tomatoes, cumin, and chili powder and layer your chips with just cheese and pico de gallo—much like the original nachos: tortillas topped with shredded cheese and pickled jalapeños, invented by a man named "Nacho."

CHICKEN GYROS

Chicken breast tenders are marinated with Mediterranean flavors, then broiled and served in warm pitas with a delicious tzatziki sauce. Serve these homemade gyros with your favorite topping, such as sliced onion, tomato, cucumber, or olives. If you don't want to use tzatziki, try hummus.

NUT-FREE

SERVES 4 TO 6
PREP TIME: 20 MINUTES, PLUS
1 HOUR TO MARINATE
COOK TIME: 12 MINUTES

EQUIPMENT:

1 gallon-size resealable bag
Bowls: small, medium
Whisk
Tongs
Grill pan or broiler pan
Meat thermometer
Paper towel
Oven mitts

INGREDIENTS:

FOR THE CHICKEN AND
THE MARINADE

1½ pounds chicken
   breast tenders
¼ cup olive oil
2 tablespoons freshly
   squeezed lemon juice
1 teaspoon dried oregano
1 teaspoon salt

 HELPING HAND: Let your helper know you'll need assistance with step 4.

1. **Prepare the chicken.**

   Put the chicken in a large resealable bag. Set it aside.

2. **Prepare the marinade.**

   In a small bowl, whisk the oil, lemon juice, oregano, and salt to combine. Pour the marinade over the chicken and seal the bag. Turn the bag to coat the chicken. Refrigerate the chicken in the marinade for at least 1 hour.

3. **Preheat the broiler.**

   About 5 minutes before you are ready to cook, position a rack in the oven close to the broiler (ask for help if you need it), and turn the broiler to high.

continued >>

FOR THE PITAS

4 to 6 whole-grain pitas

½ to ¾ cup store-bought tzatziki (found in the refrigerated section at your grocery store)

Red onion slices, for topping (optional)

Tomato slices, for topping (optional)

Crumbled feta cheese, for topping (optional)

4. **Cook.**

Using tongs, transfer the marinated chicken to an oven-safe grill pan or broiler pan. Discard the marinade. Broil the chicken for 5 minutes. Flip the chicken over and broil for 5 to 7 minutes more, or until the internal temperature reaches 165°F.

5. **Warm the pitas.**

Wet the paper towel and squeeze out any excess water. Wrap the pitas in the damp paper towel and warm them in the microwave on high power for 25 to 40 seconds before serving. Be careful when removing the pitas from the microwave (use oven mitts); they will be hot.

6. **Serve.**

Fill a warm pita with a piece of chicken and some tzatziki. Top with red onion, tomatoes, and feta cheese (if using).

MIX IT UP: Use the extra tzatziki sauce as a veggie dip!

Chocolate and Fruit Cones, page 120

CHAPTER SIX

DESSERT

CHOCOLATE AND FRUIT CONES

Chocolate-dipped, fruit-filled waffle cones make a light and delicious dessert. This recipe for handheld treats is perfect for a larger group, or you can place unfilled waffle cones in a resealable bag and pop them in the freezer for your next ice-cream treat. To make it so the cones stay upright when you serve them, place them in a colander so the pointy end is braced on one of the holes in the bottom and the top rests against the side of the colander. This helps keep the cones upright and the fruit inside the waffle cones.

30-MINUTE MEAL
NO HELP NEEDED
VEGETARIAN

SERVES 12
PREP TIME: 30 MINUTES

EQUIPMENT:
Parchment paper
Medium microwave-safe
  bowl
Measuring cups
  and spoons
Medium bowl
2 spoons
Colander

INGREDIENTS:
½ cup semisweet
  chocolate chips
½ cup butterscotch chips
12 sugar or waffle cones
1 (16-ounce) carton fresh
  strawberries, tops
  removed, sliced
1 large bunch
  seedless grapes
1 (12-ounce) carton fresh
  blueberries

1. **Prepare your workspace.**

   Line a clean work surface with parchment paper.

2. **Melt the chips.**

   In a medium microwave-safe bowl, combine the chocolate chips and butterscotch chips. Microwave on high power for 1 minute. Carefully remove the bowl from the microwave and stir the chips. Continue to microwave in 20-second increments, stirring between each, until the chips are melted.

3. **Dip the cones.**

   Dip the top of a waffle cone into the melted chocolate and butterscotch chips, and place the dipped cone on the parchment paper to set. Repeat with the remaining cones.

4. **Combine the fruit.**

   In a medium bowl, gently stir together the strawberries, grapes, and blueberries.

5. **Assemble the cones.**

   Once the coating has set on the cones (this should take about 15 minutes), spoon fruit into each cone and serve.

MIX IT UP: After dipping each waffle cone into the chocolate, roll it in sprinkles, crushed graham crackers, or crushed nuts.

CARAMEL APPLE NACHOS

You can get creative with these caramel apple nachos. Follow the recipe as-is, or create your own version using different quantities of ingredients. Swap the caramel for chocolate sauce or drizzle with peanut butter. Use red and green apples rather than pears, or use all pears. It's up to you!

| 30-MINUTE MEAL | SERVES 4 |
| VEGETARIAN | PREP TIME: 15 MINUTES |

EQUIPMENT:
Cutting board
Apple corer
Knife
Measuring cups and spoons
Serving platter

INGREDIENTS:
2 apples
2 pears
¼ cup prepared caramel sauce (heated in the microwave according to the package instructions, if you like)
2 tablespoons sweetened shredded coconut
2 tablespoons mini semisweet chocolate chips
Crushed pretzels, for topping (optional)
Granola, for topping (optional)
Dried fruit, for topping (optional)

 HELPING HAND: Let your helper know you'll need assistance with step 1.

1. **Cut the fruit.**

   On a cutting board, use an apple corer to core the apples. Cut the apples and pears into slices. Arrange the fruit slices on a serving platter.

2. **Add the sauce.**

   Drizzle the fruit with the caramel sauce.

3. **Add toppings.**

   Sprinkle the caramel with coconut, chocolate chips, and other toppings, as desired. Enjoy.

GETTING MESSY: If you want to prevent the apples and pears from browning, put the slices into a mixture of 1 tablespoon freshly squeezed lemon juice and 1 cup water. Cover and refrigerate for up to 24 hours in advance. Remove the slices and pat them dry with a paper towel. Follow the recipe as directed.

FUN FACT: Why do apples brown when they're exposed to air? It's chemistry. When an apple is damaged (such as when it is cut), the enzymes in the apple react to oxygen in the air, causing the apple to produce a compound called melanin to protect itself. This is the brown color you see. Citric acid, otherwise known as vitamin C, is found in lemon juice and deactivates the enzyme, preventing browning. But it's not only lemon juice that works to stop browning; you can also use lime juice, orange juice, or even pineapple juice.

FROYO DOTS

Dippin' Dots are one of my kids' favorite treats when we're at amusement parks. Although this recipe is not quite the same, it doesn't include liquid nitrogen (Yup, that is how the original is made!) so you can make it at home. Use your favorite flavor of yogurt, or try vanilla yogurt and add fresh or frozen fruit.

5 INGREDIENTS OR LESS
NO HELP NEEDED
NUT-FREE
VEGETARIAN

SERVES 2 TO 4
PREP TIME: 15 MINUTES, PLUS
30 MINUTES TO FREEZE

EQUIPMENT:
Baking sheet
Parchment paper
Measuring cups
   and spoons
Medium bowl
Handheld electric mixer
Spatula
Resealable bag
Clean scissors
Flipper

INGREDIENTS:
½ cup flavored yogurt
   of choice
¼ cup cream cheese, at
   room temperature
2 tablespoons
   powdered sugar

1. **Prepare a baking sheet.**

   Line a large baking sheet with parchment paper.

2. **Combine the ingredients.**

   In a medium bowl, combine the yogurt, cream cheese, and powdered sugar. Using a hand mixer, mix until all is well combined.

3. **Pipe the mixture.**

   Using a spatula, transfer the mixture to a resealable bag, press the air out, and seal the bag shut. Twist the top of the bag, pushing the mixture to the bottom of the bag, and hold the bag firmly. Snip a little bit off a bottom corner of the bag, creating a piping bag. Gently squeeze the piping bag, piping dots that are about ¼ inch wide onto the parchment. Continue piping dots until the mixture is used up, covering the parchment. (Depending on the size of your dots, this recipe makes about 50 dots.)

4. Chill.

Transfer the baking sheet to the freezer and freeze for 30 minutes. Using your hands or a flipper, remove the dots from the parchment. Serve in bowls or store in a resealable bag in the freezer.

FUN FACT: The Dippin' Dots you buy are flash frozen into tiny beads at temperatures of negative 320°F!

FROZEN S'MORES

These s'mores were developed for those times when you're not by a campfire but still have a craving for that magical combination of chocolate, marshmallow, and graham cracker. These are best served frozen but are still delicious if you can't wait that long!

5 INGREDIENTS OR LESS
NO HELP NEEDED
NUT-FREE
VEGETARIAN

SERVES 6
PREP TIME: 15 MINUTES, PLUS FREEZING TIME

EQUIPMENT:
Measuring cups
  and spoons
Small bowl
Spoon
Spatula spreader or
  cake spatula
Baking sheet

INGREDIENTS:
2 tablespoons cream
  cheese, at room
  temperature
½ cup marshmallow creme
⅓ cup chocolate frosting
6 graham crackers,
  broken in half

1. **Make the filling.**

   In a small bowl, stir together the cream cheese and marshmallow creme until well combined.

2. **Add the frosting.**

   Spread chocolate frosting on 6 graham cracker halves.

3. **Add the filling.**

   Spread the marshmallow creme mixture on the remaining 6 graham cracker halves.

4. **Assemble.**

   Gently press together one chocolate-covered and one marshmallow-covered cracker, filling-side in. Place the s'more onto a baking sheet. Repeat with the remaining crackers.

5. **Chill.**

   Freeze the s'mores for 1 to 2 hours, or eat as-is.

FUN FACT: S'mores were originally called "Some Mores."

FESTIVE DIRT CAKE

Dirt cake contains no dirt at all—but it is packed with cookies! This recipe has you smashing chocolate sandwich cookies, combining them with your favorite sprinkles, then layering with vanilla pudding and whipped topping. You can make this dessert in a pan or layer it in individual clear glass serving cups.

30-MINUTE MEAL
NO HELP NEEDED
NUT-FREE

SERVES 8
PREP TIME: 20 MINUTES

EQUIPMENT:
Large resealable bag
Rolling pin
Measuring cups
Large mixing bowl
Whisk
Spatula
9-by-9-inch baking pan

INGREDIENTS:
1 (14.3-ounce) package chocolate sandwich cookies (I like Oreos)
1 cup plain Greek yogurt
1 cup milk
1 (3.4-ounce) package instant vanilla pudding mix
1 (12-ounce) container frozen whipped topping (I like Cool Whip)
¼ cup of your favorite sprinkles (optional)

1. **Crush the cookies.**

   Put the cookies into a large resealable bag and seal the bag, pushing out as much air as you can as you go. Put the bag on a sturdy surface. Using a rolling pin or kitchen mallet, roll and crush the cookies until they resemble dirt (some larger pieces are okay). Set aside.

2. **Make the pudding mixture.**

   In a large bowl, combine the yogurt, milk, and pudding mix. Whisk for 2 minutes, or until combined and thickened.

3. **Fold in the whipped topping.**

   Using a spatula, gently fold the whipped topping into the pudding mixture just until combined.

4. **Assemble.**

In the bottom of a 9-by-9-inch pan, spread half the crushed cookies. Evenly top with the pudding mixture. Top the filling with the remaining crushed cookies.

5. **Decorate.**

Add sprinkles on top (if using).

6. **Chill.**

Cover the pan and refrigerate until you're ready to serve. Dirt cake is best served within 24 hours.

MIX IT UP: Grab a new, clean sand pail and make dirt dessert right in the bucket. Top with gummy worms for a different twist and serve with the sand scoop.

OATMEAL-CHOCOLATE CHIP COOKIE DOUGH BITES

Oatmeal-chocolate chip cookie dough bites are so good it's hard to have just one! These are perfect for an on-the-go dessert or packed in a lunchbox. Because this cookie dough is made without eggs or raw flour, these dough bites are safe to eat without cooking.

NO HELP NEEDED
NUT-FREE
VEGETARIAN

MAKES ABOUT 24 BITES
PREP TIME: 30 MINUTES, PLUS
1 HOUR TO CHILL

EQUIPMENT:
Blender or food processor
Large bowl
Measuring cups and spoons
Handheld electric mixer
Can opener
Wooden spoon
Tablespoon

INGREDIENTS:
5 cups quick cooking oats
8 tablespoons (1 stick)
  salted butter, at room
  temperature
¾ cup packed light
  brown sugar
1 teaspoon vanilla extract
½ teaspoon salt
1 (14-ounce) can sweetened
  condensed milk
½ cup mini semisweet
  chocolate chips

1. **Blend the oats.**

   In a blender or food processor, process the oats until they resemble the texture of flour. Set aside.

2. **Combine the wet ingredients.**

   In a large bowl, using a hand mixer, cream together the butter, brown sugar, vanilla, and salt (the mixture will look like sand before coming together). Add the sweetened condensed milk. Mix well.

3. **Combine the dry ingredients.**

   Add the oat flour to the wet ingredients and stir until combined. Add the chocolate chips. Mix well.

4. **Chill the dough.**

   Refrigerate the dough for 30 minutes to 1 hour.

5. **Roll the dough.**

Using a tablespoon, scoop up about 2 tablespoons of dough and roll it into a ball. Place the ball in an airtight container. Continue scooping and rolling until all of the dough is rolled. Cover the container and refrigerate the balls for up to 1 week.

MIX IT UP: Save time by spreading the finished cookie dough into a 9-by-9-inch baking pan rather than rolling it into balls. Refrigerate for 30 minutes before cutting into squares.

GABBY'S DOUBLE CHOCOLATE RICE TREAT BARS

My daughter, Gabby, is obsessed with chocolate-hazelnut spread. We always have a jar in our pantry, which made it the perfect fit for super chocolatey puffed rice bars. These bars are made in the microwave and come together in about 10 minutes!

5 INGREDIENTS OR LESS
NO HELP NEEDED

SERVES 12
PREP TIME: 15 MINUTES
COOK TIME: 1 MINUTE

EQUIPMENT:
9-by-9-inch baking pan
Measuring cups
  and spoons
Medium bowl
Large microwave-safe bowl
Butter knife
Wooden spoon

INGREDIENTS:
Nonstick cooking spray
4 cups chocolate puffed
  rice cereal (Cocoa Rice
  Krispies work well)
3 cups mini marshmallows
½ cup chocolate-hazelnut
  spread (such as Nutella)
2 tablespoons salted
  butter, cut into 4 cubes

1. **Grease the pan.**

   Coat a 9-by-9-inch pan with cooking spray. Set it aside.

2. **Prep the cereal.**

   Put the puffed rice cereal in a medium bowl. Set it aside.

3. **Prepare the marshmallow mixture.**

   In a large microwave-safe bowl, combine the marshmallows, chocolate-hazelnut spread, and butter cubes.

4. **Microwave the marshmallow mixture.**

   Put the marshmallow mixture in the microwave and cook on high power for 1 minute. Stir well. If the marshmallows are not melted, continue to microwave in 10-second increments, stirring between each, until the marshmallows are completely melted.

continued >>

5. Combine.

As soon as the marshmallows are melted, add them to the puffed rice cereal and stir until the cereal is completely coated.

6. Assemble.

Pour the cereal mixture into the prepared baking pan. Coat your clean hands with cooking spray and, using your greased hands, gently press the cereal mixture down to flatten it. Let it cool completely before slicing into 12 squares.

FUN FACT: Each 13-ounce jar of Nutella, the most popular brand of chocolate-hazelnut spread, contains 50 hazelnuts.

STRAWBERRY-BANANA SHERBET

My kids are always asking to make ice cream but we never seem to have the ingredients on hand. This version is made with freezer and pantry items in a blender and is packed with fruit, resulting in a creamy sherbet that everyone loves.

NO HELP NEEDED
VEGETARIAN

SERVES 4
PREP TIME: 10 MINUTES, PLUS
3 HOURS TO FREEZE

EQUIPMENT:
Blender or food processor
Measuring cups
  and spoons
Loaf pan
Spatula
Ice-cream scoop

INGREDIENTS:
3 cups frozen strawberries
1 overripe banana, frozen
¾ cup sweetened
  condensed milk
1 teaspoon freshly
  squeezed lemon juice
½ teaspoon almond extract
  or vanilla extract
Dash salt

1. **Puree the fruit.**

   In a blender or food processor, combine the frozen strawberries, banana, sweetened condensed milk, lemon juice, almond extract, and salt. Puree until smooth, stopping to scrape down the sides of the blender with a spatula, as needed, to ensure all the berries are pureed.

2. **Freeze.**

   Pour the mixture into a loaf pan, spreading it with the spatula. Freeze for 2 to 3 hours, or until the mixture reaches a sherbet consistency and can be scooped.

   MIX IT UP: Instead of the banana, try 2 cups strawberries and 1½ cups frozen blueberries, raspberries, or mango!

VANILLA CONFETTI MUG CAKE

This individual serving of cake is baked in the microwave in less than 2 minutes!
Make the cake festive for any occasion by using colorful sprinkles.

10 MINUTES OR LESS
NO HELP NEEDED
NUT-FREE
VEGETARIAN

SERVES 1
PREP TIME: 10 MINUTES
COOK TIME:
1 MINUTE 20 SECONDS

EQUIPMENT:
Large microwave-safe mug
2 small bowls
Measuring cups and spoons
Fork
Spoon
Oven mitts

INGREDIENTS:
Nonstick cooking spray
1 large egg yolk (see step 2)
2 tablespoons sugar
1 tablespoon vegetable oil
1 tablespoon unsweetened
  applesauce
1 tablespoon milk
½ teaspoon vanilla extract
¼ cup all-purpose flour
½ teaspoon baking powder
⅛ teaspoon salt
1 teaspoon confetti sprinkles
Whipped cream, vanilla
  ice cream, or frosting, for
  serving (optional)

1. **Prepare the mug.**

   Coat a large microwave-safe mug with cooking spray.

2. **Separate the yolk from the white.**

   Crack the egg in the middle over a small bowl but do not pull it apart yet. Holding one half of the shell in each hand, carefully pour the egg yolk back and forth into each half of the shell until only the yellow yolk remains in the shell and the whites are in the bowl. Put the yolk in the prepared mug.

3. **Combine the wet ingredients.**

   To the mug, add the sugar, oil, applesauce, milk, and vanilla. Mix well with a fork.

4. **Combine the dry ingredients.**

   In a small bowl, stir together the flour, baking powder, and salt. Add the dry ingredients to the wet ingredients and stir well. Stir in the sprinkles.

   continued >>

5. **Cook the cake.**

Microwave the mug on high power for 1 minute and 20 seconds until the batter is cooked. Using oven mitts, carefully remove the mug from the microwave. Let the mug cake cool for 1 minute.

6. **Garnish.**

Top as desired.

MIX IT UP: To make chocolate mug cake, stir in 1 tablespoon cocoa powder and 1 tablespoon mini chocolate chips in step 4.

GETTING MESSY: Be sure to use a large mug. The cake might spill over the top of a standard-size coffee mug while cooking. Alternatively, you could use a small microwave-safe bowl to cook your cake.

WHOLE-WHEAT CHOCOLATE CHIP MONKEY MUFFINS

Did you know that as bananas get browner on the outside, the banana gets sweeter? The starch inside bananas breaks down into sugar. This makes overripe bananas *perfect* for muffins. This recipe combines the sweetness of super-ripe bananas with chocolate chips in a delicious muffin that is great for dessert or an after-school treat.

30-MINUTE MEAL
NUT-FREE
VEGETARIAN

MAKES 12 MUFFINS
PREP TIME: 10 MINUTES
BAKE TIME: 20 MINUTES

EQUIPMENT:
Muffin pan
Bowls: large, medium
Fork
Measuring cups and spoons
Whisk
Spatula
Wooden spoon
Oven mitts
Toothpicks

INGREDIENTS:
Nonstick cooking spray
3 overripe bananas
½ cup sugar
½ cup unsweetened
  applesauce
1 large egg
1 teaspoon vanilla extract
2 cups whole-wheat flour

 HELPING HAND: Let your helper know you'll need assistance with step 7.

1. **Preheat the oven to 400°F.**

   Coat a 12-cup muffin pan with cooking spray. Set it aside.

2. **Smash the bananas.**

   In a large bowl, using a fork, smash the bananas until they are mostly smooth.

3. **Combine the wet ingredients.**

   To the bananas, add the sugar, applesauce, egg, and vanilla. Stir well to mix.

4. **Combine the dry ingredients.**

   In a medium bowl, whisk the flour, cinnamon, baking soda, and salt to blend.

continued >>

2 teaspoons ground
  cinnamon
1 teaspoon baking soda
½ teaspoon salt
½ cup semisweet
  chocolate chips

5. **Combine the wet and dry ingredients.**

   Add the flour mixture to the banana mixture and stir until just combined.

6. **Add the chocolate chips.**

   Using a wooden spoon, fold in the chocolate chips.

7. **Bake.**

   Evenly divide the batter among the prepared muffin cups. Transfer the pan to the preheated oven and bake for 20 minutes, or until a toothpick inserted into the center of a muffin comes out clean. Let the muffins cool completely on a wire rack.

MIX IT UP: When you have overripe bananas, don't throw them out. Either peel them and seal them in a freezer bag or pop the whole banana into the freezer, peel and all. Frozen bananas work great in baked goods. Simply set the frozen bananas on the counter to thaw, then use as directed. They won't look appetizing, but they work great.

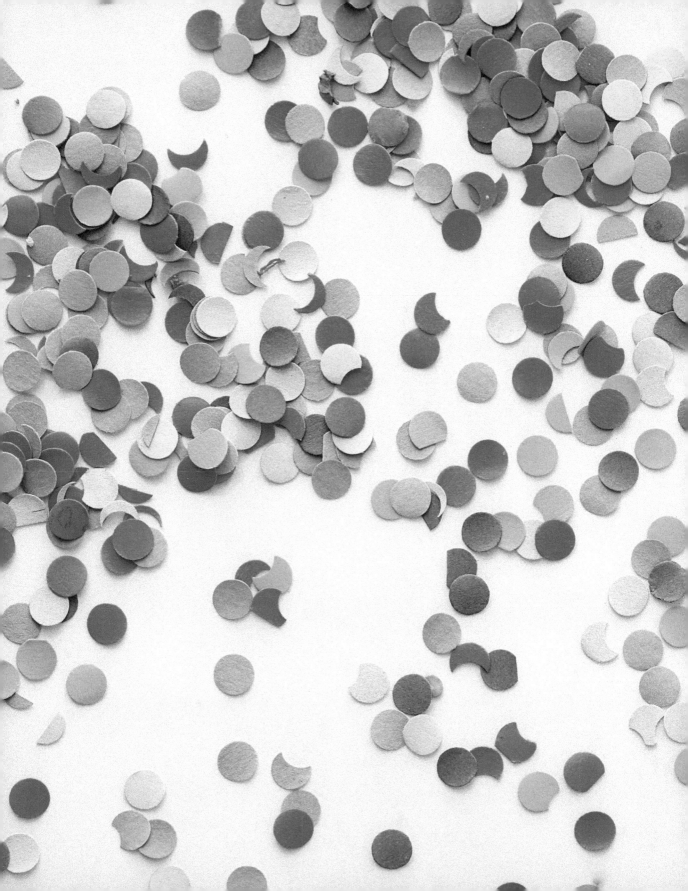

CONVERSION TABLES

WEIGHT EQUIVALENTS

US STANDARD	METRIC (APPROXIMATE)
½ ounce	15 g
1 ounce	30 g
2 ounces	60 g
4 ounces	115 g
8 ounces	225 g
12 ounces	340 g
16 ounces or 1 pound	455 g

OVEN TEMPERATURES

FAHRENHEIT (F)	CELSIUS (C) (APPROXIMATE)
250°F	120°C
300°F	150°C
325°F	165°C
350°F	180°C
375°F	190°C
400°F	200°C
425°F	220°C
450°F	230°C

VOLUME EQUIVALENTS (LIQUID)

US STANDARD	US STANDARD (OUNCES)	METRIC (APPROXIMATE)
2 tablespoons	1 fl. oz.	30 mL
¼ cup	2 fl. oz.	60 mL
½ cup	4 fl. oz.	120 mL
1 cup	8 fl. oz.	240 mL
1½ cups	12 fl. oz.	355 mL
2 cups or 1 pint	16 fl. oz.	475 mL
4 cups or 1 quart	32 fl. oz.	1 L
1 gallon	128 fl. oz.	4 L

VOLUME EQUIVALENTS (DRY)

US STANDARD	METRIC (APPROXIMATE)
⅛ teaspoon	0.5 mL
¼ teaspoon	1 mL
½ teaspoon	2 mL
¾ teaspoon	4 mL
1 teaspoon	5 mL
1 tablespoon	15 mL
¼ cup	59 mL
⅓ cup	79 mL
½ cup	118 mL
⅔ cup	156 mL
¾ cup	177 mL
1 cup	235 mL
2 cups or 1 pint	475 mL
3 cups	700 mL
4 cups or 1 quart	1 L

DIFFICULTY INDEX

LABEL INDEX

INDEX

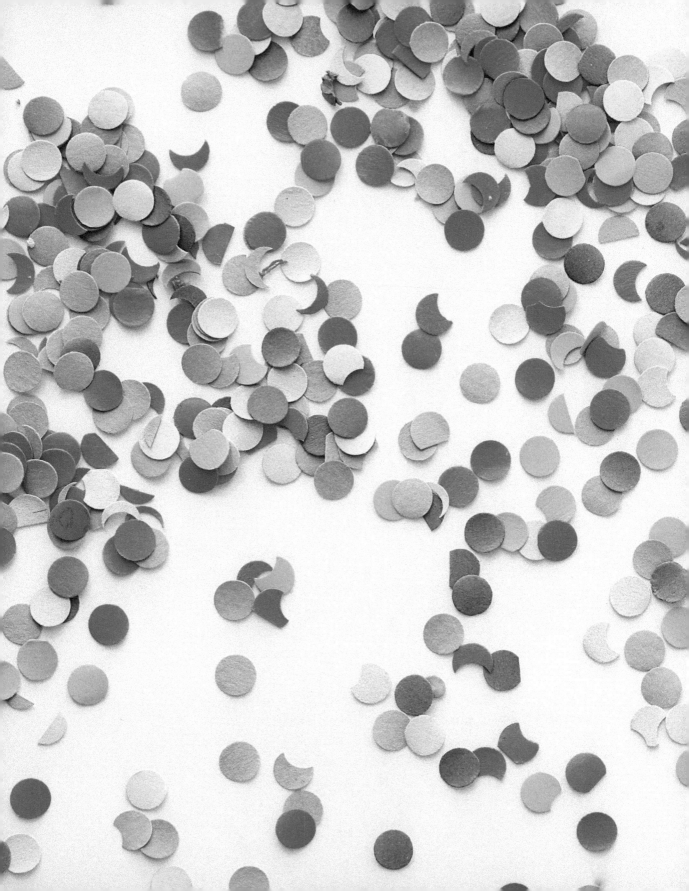

ACKNOWLEDGMENTS

I wouldn't be in this line of work if things hadn't fallen as they did throughout my life's path. I've been inspired by many, starting in childhood watching the tireless dedication my mom had for feeding our family homemade meals every day, going so far as to plan out 2 weeks' worth of wayside and campground meals for a road trip one summer. I believe watching her sit at our kitchen table, time and time again, planning nutritious, homemade meals—and always eating as a family—played a part in my interest in food and nutrition, and therefore my bachelor of science degree in dietetics.

My nutrition path started in renal nutrition, then I decided to become a stay-at-home mom. I'll forever cherish my memories cooking along with my children as babies, then toddlers; helping them grow into budding chefs and now skilled cooks even at their young ages.

I'm thankful my path back to the working world was writing lunch menus and feeding Pre-K through eighth-grade children (including my own!) at Notre Dame of De Pere Elementary and Middle School. This sparked my interest and gave me the confidence to launch Create Kids Club.

I quickly learned that the online world was a whole new space I wasn't prepared to undertake on my own. I will be forever grateful to the amazing women and fellow dietitians at Blog Brûlée for selecting me and for their belief in Create Kids Club. You certainly helped me "set my blog on fire!"

Lastly, I'm so very appreciative and grateful to the readers and followers of Create Kids Club who inspire me daily to continue on my path toward helping families enjoy homemade meals together more often, because I believe this simple act impacts kids' lives forever.

ABOUT THE AUTHOR

Jodi Danen, RDN, is a registered dietitian with nearly 20 years of experience in the food, nutrition, and culinary communications area. She has appeared across many media outlets including TV, podcasts, and publications, and she developed Lunch Bites lunchbox notecards.

Jodi is passionate about helping kids and adults learn to feel comfortable in the kitchen. She has dedicated her career to helping families come together around the dinner table enjoying nutritious and delicious home-made meals. Jodi offers simple family-friendly recipes and vacation ideas on her food and travel site, Create Kids Club (CreateKidsClub.com). She enjoys making and sharing videos that make cooking her recipes simple and straightforward. This is her first cookbook.

Jodi lives in Green Bay, Wisconsin, with her sous-chefs: her 12-year-old daughter (a budding artist) and her 14-year-old son (solver of all tech problems), along with her pizza-loving husband (and number-one fan) and their adorable, and sometimes sassy, golden retriever.

Follow her on social media @CreateKidsClub.

Printed in the USA
CPSIA information can be obtained
at www.ICGtesting.com
LVHW081657301123
764704LV00004B/60